CONSENT, FREEDOM
AND
POLITICAL OBLIGATION

BY

J. P. PLAMENATZ

Chichele Professor of Social and
Political Theory in the
University of Oxford

SECOND EDITION

OXFORD UNIVERSITY PRESS

LONDON   OXFORD   NEW YORK

1968

Oxford University Press

OXFORD LONDON NEW YORK
GLASGOW TORONTO MELBOURNE WELLINGTON
CAPE TOWN SALISBURY IBADAN NAIROBI LUSAKA ADDIS ABABA
BOMBAY CALCUTTA MADRAS KARACHI LAHORE DACCA
KUALA LUMPUR HONG KONG TOKYO

First published in the
Oxford Classical and Philosophical Monographs series
1938
Second edition, first published as an
Oxford University Press paperback
1968

PRINTED IN GREAT BRITAIN

PREFACE TO THE SECOND EDITION

IN preparing the main text of this book for the second edition, I have confined myself to making verbal alterations. I have made no attempt to improve its arguments, even the weakest of them, nor to soften its criticisms, even the most inept. A book written a long time ago may or may not be worth republishing, but if it is republished, let it be so with little correction and less apology. I have, however, added a final chapter to give the reader some idea of what I now think about matters I discussed some thirty years ago.

Oxford 1967   J. P. P.

PREFACE TO THE FIRST EDITION

THE extent of my indebtedness to contemporary writers on Moral and Political Philosophy, and to all those who have treated of matters relevant to this inquiry, more particularly to Professor Moore, Professor Prichard, Sir David Ross, and Mr. Carritt, will be easily apparent to whoever reads this book.

But I am, above all, indebted to Mr. W. G. Maclagan of Oriel College, who has discussed almost every point of importance with me, and who has helped me to express myself much more clearly than I might otherwise have done.

Sir David Ross has read through this book both in manuscript and in proof. I must thank him for a large number of important suggestions and corrections.

J. P. P.

CONTENTS

INTRODUCTION

THE purpose of this book is to provide definitions of a number of words generally used by political thinkers, and to discover whether the duty of the governed to obey their governments is, on the whole, greater in proportion to the extent to which the latter act with the consent of the former. The attempt to define and to justify the definitions of three words, 'consent', 'freedom', and 'rights', takes up the greater part of the book, but it is obviously necessary to be clear as to what they mean before it is possible adequately to fulfil the other part of our purpose.

No definitions are offered of such words as 'good', 'right', and 'ought', though they are constantly used and also form part of the three major definitions given. It is necessary, therefore, to point out that such use cannot bind the user to any particular interpretation of them. The arguments advanced in this book, however weak or however strong they may be, do not stand or fall with any particular theory of the nature of goodness or moral obligation. The subjectivist who explains all moral notions in psychological terms has as good a right to the use of such words as 'good' and 'ought' as any one else, provided that he makes his position clear and finds the words convenient. None of Professor Moore's arguments directed against the naturalistic fallacy really prove what they set out to prove, though this is no evidence of the falseness of his major thesis. We are all constantly guilty of uttering tautologies under the conviction that we are not doing so. No argument, therefore, which finally reduces to the contention that, if 'good' meant 'approved of' or any other relational property, certain statements would be tautologies which certainly do not appear to be so, need worry the subjectivist. And this, it must be remembered, is the only kind of argument that can be brought against him. He has only to reply that, since synonyms are many and human intelligence is weak, it is not unlikely that there can be found philosophers who passionately deny that A is A. But, of course, the subjectivist's position is no stronger than his opponent's. Most of the arguments in this book apply, whatever the correct interpretation of the words 'good' and 'right'. A few, included for the sake of completeness, apply only if views such as Professor Moore holds are correct.

An attempt to define 'consent' naturally leads one to a consideration of the Idealist account of political obligation, which is the most complete attempt ever made to found it entirely upon *consent*. It will be shown that this attempt must, on Idealist premises, defeat itself, since it makes consent both impossible and unnecessary. This theory, but not primarily as a theory of consent, was criticized by Professor Hobhouse in his *Metaphysical Theory of the State*. But his criticism is not altogether satisfactory, because the effectiveness of many of its details depends upon serious misinterpretations of Hegelian political philosophy.

Some of the chief contentions advanced by the Idealists, when stated in clear and simple language, are so manifestly absurd that many people must be astonished to think that there ever existed intellectually eminent persons who could persuade themselves of their truth. An attempt has been made throughout this book to show that many of these contentions are merely everyday metaphors taken literally. And it must not be forgotten that there is a strong tendency in every human mind to treat metaphors in this way. It was a tendency which was even stronger, perhaps, in the philosophers of ancient Greece than in those of modern Europe, with the exception, of course, of the Hegelians, who made the most intransigent of all known attempts to convert a number of poetically effective ambiguities into a logical system. But it must not be forgotten that some of the thinkers most deeply affected by this disease made many of the shrewdest and most penetrating remarks.

INTRODUCTION ix

It may appear that some of the arguments in this book are developed at too great a length, and that brevity would have made them more clear. This is a fault which it is sometimes difficult to avoid, since no one wishes to appear hasty or superficial in his conclusions. Moreover, the very anxiety to be as unambiguous as possible sometimes leads the writer into excessive complexity in the putting of quite simple points. But the best of all excuses for this manner of proceeding is to be found in the historical fact that a great deal of apparently clear and simple exposition covers up ambiguities and false arguments, which go unperceived for the very reason that strict accuracy, which often involves complexity of statement, is sacrificed to other more attractive qualities. It is feared, nevertheless, that this book contains inaccuracies and false arguments presented in a style which only the enunciation of important truths could excuse.

The definition of freedom offered in this book avoids the old controversy between Determinists and Indeterminists. It has been thought best to avoid taking sides in a quarrel in which, in the last analysis, it may turn out that there are no sides to take. Many persons find the greatest difficulty in attaching any meaning to the *spontaneous choice* of the Indeterminist. Others deny the self-evidence of the causal law, even when it is enunciated as a mere law of necessary succession and concomitance. Indeed, some philosophers insist that it is absurd to apply the notion of necessity to the order of occurrences in the world. Whatever his personal opinion, whoever has had occasion to discover the extraordinary difficulty of producing a satisfactory formulation of an allegedly self-evident law will agree that a writer on politics has every excuse for avoiding an obscure controversy, which, whatever its ultimate outcome, is not likely to help him in the solution of the much less attractive, but also much less difficult, problems which interest him.

Marxist thinkers have always pointed out, with special emphasis, that the word 'freedom' has been used in many different meanings, but they have enormously exaggerated their number, trying to persuade themselves and others that the freedom to perform one kind of action is a different kind of freedom from the freedom to perform another. This, of course, is an obviously false contention, and it is not worth our while to deal with it at any length. Its truth would involve the existence of as many 'freedoms' as there are qualitatively distinguishable actions, since no mention is made of the degree of determinateness which a class of actions must possess before the freedom to perform them can acquire the status of a separate sort of freedom. This is not to deny, of course, that Marx had very good reason for saying that working-men enjoy considerably less freedom than their employers. But this is another question, of far greater practical importance, no doubt, but for our purposes quite irrelevant.

This book, indeed, claims to be purely theoretical. It is concerned to do nothing more than to attempt definitions of several words often used in political discussions, and to discover in what ways the facts which they mean are related to each other. No such knowledge can help any one to solve any practical problem whatsoever, except to the extent to which clear thinking on abstract matters is desirable to this end. But it must be conceded that, as a matter of fact, many of the most practical men are the most muddle-headed; some of them, like Lenin, being apparently incapable of expressing themselves on theoretical matters with even an ordinary amount of clarity and sense.

It should also be clear that any discussion of Marxist criticisms of the present form of society would be out of place in a book of this kind. Whatever the existing form of social and economic organization, however men come by their opinions, and however much their having the particular opinions which they have may enable a minority of them to exploit the others, the words 'consent', 'right', and 'freedom' continue to have the same meanings, except to the extent to which changes in their linguistic habits cause men to mean a different fact by a given sound at one time from what they mean by it at another. Marxists should be pleased to think that the victims of capitalism mean the same thing by freedom as they do themselves, for unless this were so they would find it harder to point out to them the error of their ways.

The 'philosophical' foundation which Marx supposed that he provided for his social, political, and economic principles has long been known to be the weakest part of his writings, whose strength lies not in their logical completeness and clarity of exposition, but in the remarkable shrewdness with which he attacked the existing system at its weakest points. So that, though it has been thought superfluous to waste time on the very easy business of pulling to pieces phrases which have been very often ridiculed without losing any of their power to cast a spell on the faithful, this should not be taken as a sign of agreement with those who believe that the main force of Marx's indictment of the existing form of society stands or falls with them.

This book contains more statements of the obvious than some readers will like. Political philosophy is a subject in which most exciting and paradoxical statements are either false or meaningless. Platitudes must be repeated frequently, more by way of protest than for the sake of information.

INDEX OF PROPER NAMES

The philosophical and political terms which are discussed in this book, and not merely used, are so few in number and occur so frequently, that it would serve no useful purpose to include them in the index. The titles of the chapters, together with the names of philosophers and political writers included in this index, should serve as a sufficient guide.

CHAPTER I

CONSENT

THE main purpose of this book is to inquire into and to attempt to define the relations between consent, freedom, and the duty of the governed to obey their rulers. But before the inquiry can be begun it is necessary to avoid all ambiguity as to the meanings of the words which describe its nature. Now the word 'consent' has been used in many meanings, and part of the purpose of this chapter will be to attempt a definition of that one of its meanings which makes the phrase 'government by consent' synonymous with representative government. This statement should make it clear that no arbitrary definition will be attempted, but rather that of the only meaning of the word which is relevant to the inquiry which is the subject of this book. Nothing so absurd as the claim that people ought to give any particular meaning to the word will be advanced. Our only object will be to discover what they actually mean by it in the meaning relevant to this inquiry, and the word 'ought' will, in this connexion, be used as an hypothetical imperative. If people wish to be intelligible and to advance valid arguments, they ought not to pass from one meaning of a word to another, nor assume that what is true of the first is also true of the second.

There will be nothing arbitrary in our method of arriving at the definition we require. It will be very similar to that adopted by Socrates in his search for a definition of justice. If, then, the final definition appears so narrow as to make it appear that no actual government ever acts with the consent of all its subjects, and very seldom with the consent of even a majority of them, it is not permissible, for that reason, to conclude that the definition is wrong. For the mere fact that we find ourselves obliged to accept certain unpleasant conclusions is not of itself any indication of the falseness of our premisses. This elementary contention might seem obvious, and its statement appear unnecessary. But it must not be forgotten that most English political writers have, since the end of the seventeenth century, taken a paternal and proprietary interest in such words as 'consent' and 'freedom', and have not wished their meanings to be greatly restricted.

The method here used will, however, differ from that of Socrates in one respect. It will begin by giving a not altogether accurate definition of the word, and then go on to offer a criticism of some of the more usual ways in which it has been abused. This criticism of the abuses of the term will be intended to serve the same purpose as Socrates' criticism of the definitions of justice advanced by his Sophist opponents. It will be intended to prepare the ground for the final definition, which we believe to be accurate and to be a real analysis of what people actually mean by the word 'consent' in the phrase 'government by consent'.

The abuses which will be criticized in this chapter are chiefly those which recommended themselves to the Contract Philosophers. It is true, of course, that the nineteenth-century Idealists, taking their inspiration from Rousseau, also based their general political theory on a misuse of the word 'consent', but the whole doctrine of the existence of a *general* or *real will* is so complicated that we must devote an entire chapter to it. For the present it will be found more convenient to attend only to the more usual abuses of the term, which are found to be, most of them, just as common in ordinary speech as in the writings of the Contract theorists. These abuses are abuses, not because they are cases where one word is used in several meanings, but because those guilty of them, particularly political thinkers, talk as if they supposed that the word had only one meaning in each case. It is this supposition, and this supposition only, which constitutes the danger, for it is only when people are not aware that they are using the same word in different meanings that they are in danger of passing unconsciously from one meaning to another and thus of assuming that what is true of the fact referred to in the former case is also true of the one referred to in the latter.

When what is believed to be an approximately correct definition of the relevant meaning of the word has been given, and when some of its more usual abuses have been criticized, the chapter will end with an accurate definition, and with a consideration of how far the two best-known forms of popular government, direct and representative democracy, can properly be said to be based upon consent. That is to say, an attempt will be made to estimate the extent to which the laws enforced and the acts done by governments of these two kinds are enforced and done with the consent of the governed.

Should it appear that even these two forms of government are only to a limited extent governments by consent, it will necessarily follow either that consent is not the sole basis of the duty of the governed to obey their rulers or else that there exists in every state, however democratic, a large number of persons under no obligation to obey its laws. The latter conclusion is suspect from the start, for no state could perform its proper functions if it contained a large number of citizens exempt from obedience to its laws. There remains, therefore, only the former conclusion, that consent cannot be the sole basis of the duty in question, though it may well be one of them.

Let us begin, then, with a nearly accurate definition of the word 'consent'. A man's consent is always to the action or actions of another man or men. It involves on his part the expression of a wish that another or others should perform or abstain from a certain action or actions. But, at the same time, it involves more than this, for one man may express a wish that another should perform a certain action, the other may perform it, and yet the wish, in the opinion of ordinary men, may not partake of the nature of consent. The expressed wish on the part of an Indian that the Imperial Parliament should grant his country a constitution, followed by such a grant on the part of the Imperial Parliament, would not give to the Indian's wish the nature of consent. Nor yet would his wish imply consent if one of the main motives influencing the Imperial Parliament were the desire to meet this wish. It would imply consent only if the expression of the wish were the condition of the possession by the Imperial Parliament of the right to act as it does. We have consent, therefore, whenever the right of one man to act in a certain way is conditional upon another man's having expressed the wish that he should act in that way.

The man whose right to perform an action flows not merely from his own wish to perform it, nor from the thought that when it is performed it will please another, but from the fact that another has expressed the wish that he should perform it, can be called the agent of the person who has expressed the wish. He is not his agent if his action is performed for the sake of the other, i.e. in order to promote the good of the other, whether or not the other has expressed the wish that it should be performed. He is his agent only if his right to do what in fact he does depends upon the other's consent.

We do not intend at this stage in our argument to make clear just what the nature of this right is. Before we can do this we must give a definition of what we believe a *right* to be—a task which is reserved for a later chapter. But this at least can be asserted, that the right in question need not be a legal right (i.e. a power granted to a man by the supreme law-making authority); it may be a right in no way dependent upon law; that is, it may be a power which a man ought to have, whether or not it is granted to him by law. Most people agree that there are such rights, and their existence will be justified at a later stage.[1]

---

[1] The belief that all moral notions can be reduced to psychological terms

We must pass on now to a consideration of some of the other meanings of the word 'consent' which are often confused with the definition just advanced. For instance, it is sometimes thought that the fact that one man's power to perform an action depends upon other men's wishes that he should perform it, or at least upon the absence on their part of wishes that he should not perform it, makes him their agent. But it is clear that, in the meaning of the word defined above, they do not consent to his action merely because, as a matter of fact, he could not have performed it had they not wanted him to do so or had they wanted him not to do so. The view that *consent* involves no more than that a man's power to act should depend on the absence of the wish, on the part of those *consenting*, that he should not do what he intends to do, leads to many curious conclusions. For it then becomes quite reasonable to contend that a despot is governing with the consent of the governed, so long as the latter are too brutish and too ignorant to wish him to do otherwise, and so long as this brutishness and ignorance are conditions of his power to govern.

Again, apart from the question of power, it is not correct to say that persons consent to a man's action when they approve of its effects. Yet it is often said of the governed that they are consenting parties to the actions of their rulers, when these latter do what they wish them to do, or when the effects of what they do are approved of by them. Now, if this were true, it would necessarily follow that God governs the universe with the consent of the faithful, for the faithful would hardly deserve that name if they did not approve of God's actions. Moreover, He might even be said, on certain occasions, to rule with the consent of atheists, so long as they approved of the effects of His actions, although they do not know them for what they are and believe them to have a cause other than the will of God.

does not affect this issue. Those who hold this belief can still, and indeed must, distinguish a power from a right, and a legal from a moral right.

It is very unlikely that the persons who confuse consent to another's action with approval of its effects would care to allow that the two cases mentioned above can properly be described as *consent*. But if these two cannot be so described, neither can any other similar cases, so that it necessarily follows that consent to a man's action is quite distinct from approval of its effects.

Further, it cannot be said that an action which a man performs because he knows that another wishes him to perform it (whether or not his power to perform it depends upon this other's wish) is done with the consent of the latter. A child may wish to be given a particular toy by his father, and his father knowing precisely what the child wants, and moved solely by the desire to give it him, may in fact do so. It would seem that in this instance also it would be a mere abuse of language to say that the gift was made with the consent of the child. Yet many people talk as though a monarch like Elizabeth acted with the consent of her subjects, for no better reason than that she often did what they wanted her to do because she knew that they wanted her to do it.

The most curious of all cases of alleged *consent* is to be found in the writings of the Contract Philosophers, who went so far as to assert that a man, by merely inhabiting or owning property in the dominions ruled over by a government, thereby *tacitly* consented to all its laws. Locke informs us that

'every man that hath any possession or enjoyment of any part of the dominions of any government doth hereby give his tacit consent, and is as far forth obliged to obedience to the laws of that government, during this enjoyment, as anyone under it, whether this possession be of land to him and heirs forever, or a lodging for only a week; or whether it be barely travelling freely on the highway; and, in effect, it reaches as far as the very being of anyone within the territories of that government.'[1]

[1] Locke, *Second Treatise on Civil Government*, § 119.

Locke assumes that a man by merely travelling within the territories of the King of England *actually*, though *tacitly*, agrees to obey his laws. It follows then that a journey in England constitutes a promise to obey the King's laws. The promise is tacit because it is not expressed in words, orally or in writing, but it is none the less a promise. The word 'tacit' cannot alter the nature of the consent; it can only indicate the manner of its expression. Either there has been consent or there has not. Locke believes that there has.

It should not, however, be difficult to understand that travel in England is not equivalent to a promise to obey the King's laws. It does not even imply that the traveller is willing to obey them, though, even if it did so, willingness to obey the laws would not be the same thing as consent to their enforcement.

That the being inside the territories of a government does not imply a willingness to obey its laws becomes evident as soon as we consider the nature of crimes and conspiracies. Thistlewood and his associates lived and travelled in this country for many months after they had decided to attempt the destruction of its government. It is most improbable that their presence in Cato Street *implied*[1] a willingness on their part to obey all the laws administered by the men they plotted to assassinate. And yet, if Locke's argument is valid, we must presume that even Guy Fawkes's presence in the cellars of Westminster Palace implied a willingness on his part that the laws against Papists then included in the Statute Book should be enforced.

Locke, in attempting to found rightful government upon consent, imagined that he was attacking the foundations of tyranny. His attack was made with the bluntest of weapons. If consent can be *implied* by some of the things that he maintains *imply* it, then there never existed any govern-

---

[1] The word 'implied' is not, in this context, synonymous with 'entailed' in the sense in which G. E. Moore uses it. It must mean 'causally connected' in such a way that Thistlewood's presence in England could be taken as evidence of his willingness to obey the British Government.

ment but ruled with the unanimous and continuous consent of all its subjects.

The word 'tacit' has always proved useful to persons who have found it necessary to treat a word with several meanings as if it had one meaning only. It has enabled them to speak as if one fact, though it appears different from another, were really exactly similar to it and might be treated as such by persons who have sufficient shrewdness to notice the similarity. There are in all ages and in all languages a number of such words, especially useful to persons who are anxious to simplify and systematize what might otherwise prove beyond simplification and system. Students of philosophy, from the very nature of their profession, are more easily tempted, or, rather, deceived, by these words than are any other sort of men. It was certainly either a philosopher or a lawyer who first discovered that to live in a country constituted a consent to the enforcement of its laws, and then went on to make his discovery more palatable to the incredulous by adding that the consent, after all, was only tacit.

But a word, though misused, still has its proper use. There is, in spite of the philosophers, such a thing as *tacit consent*. It is tacit not because it is something which is not consent that philosophers are trying to pass off as if it were, but because it is not expressed by word of mouth, nor in writing, nor by any other action, but rather by inaction. Whenever silence may legitimately be regarded as acquiescence, and whenever such acquiescence constitutes the granting of a permission, we have an actual case of tacit consent. Any action or inaction may serve as an expression of consent so long as some such expression is necessary before the person to whom it is addressed can have the right to perform the action in question, and so long as it is made with the intention of informing him that the giver does permit him to perform it.

This last qualification must be made in order to make it

clear that the mere expression of a wish by one man that a certain action should be performed does not amount to the giving of a permission to another to perform it, even if the former had the right to give such a permission. If we suppose for the sake of argument that Henry II had the right to have St. Thomas à Becket put to death, yet the knights who murdered him were not acting with the King's consent, though they might quite plausibly have argued that his exclamation 'Who will rid me of this turbulent priest?' implied a desire on his part that some one should murder the Archbishop. The expression of desire which constitutes a proper case of consent must be a real grant of permission, that is to say it must be made with the intention of informing another or others that they have been endowed with the right to perform a certain action. So long as it is made and is known to be made with this intention, its actual form is a matter of indifference. It may consist in an oral or written statement, in a nod of the head, in a wave of the hand, or in any other convenient action. It may, as we have pointed out, consist even in silence, so long as the silence is intended and known to be a grant of permission or, in other words, a tacit consent.

It should not be alleged that consent can be given to anything but another's action, for giving one's consent means nothing more than granting to another the right to act in a certain way. If an assembly of the people decides, by a majority vote, that such-and-such a rule of action should become law, what it is consenting to (or at least what the majority of it is consenting to) is not the existence of the rule of action but its enforcement by the magistrates. The rule of action, as a way in which people's actions might be controlled, is not anything to which the majority of the assembly can consent. What it does in giving consent is merely to grant to the magistrates authority to apply rules, which is the very essence of what is known as legislation. The giving of *consent* is essentially the granting of *permission*, and there cannot be action by permission unless the right of the agent to act depends for its existence upon the granting of permission.

If we have regard to the proper meaning of the word 'permission', we must conclude that it can be granted only by one person to another. It is true that people often talk of 'permitting themselves' a luxury, as though they were creating in themselves the right to the possession or enjoyment of it. But this is to use the word in quite a different sense from the one which is relevant in a discussion of consent. In this context, to 'permit oneself a luxury' is merely to decide to enjoy something which one is not in the habit of enjoying. Otherwise to permit something is merely to consent to its existence in so far as it is brought into existence by the activities of other people.

Very often a man says of himself, 'I have consented to do such-and-such a thing', so that it appears that what he has consented to is not the action of another but his own. Here again it is clear that the word 'consent' is used in a different sense from that in which it is used when it is said that a man consents to the marriage of his daughter. The first man, when he consents, is merely making a promise, whereas the second is granting a permission to another person to act in a certain way. It cannot be said that the Prime Minister when he consents to make a speech in the Town Hall at Oxford is giving himself permission to make the speech. Far from creating a right in himself, he is merely creating an obligation. On the other hand, the father who consents to his daughter's marriage is giving her the right to do a certain action, it being presumed that she would not have the right to do it unless he first gave his consent. For if she already had the right (e.g. if she were already over twenty-one years of age) he could not, in the sense of the word relevant to this discussion, be said to be giving his consent at all.

So far we have dealt with cases of alleged consent which,

upon analysis, have proved to be nothing of the kind. We must now consider an exactly opposite contention, which maintains that the citizens of a modern state, to the extent to which they are not aware of their best interests, are not consenting parties to their governors' actions even when they voted them into power in order that they should perform them. It is often suggested by communists that the governors of a capitalistic state so corrupt the minds of the poor that they are thus artificially induced to desire the maintenance of an economic and social system which involves their exploitation. The schools and the churches teach them a capitalistic morality; the newspapers, the wireless, the cinema, and the popular novel all serve to arouse in their minds beliefs and, consequently, desires, whose existence is the first condition of the prosperity of the propertied class. The minds of the labouring poor are enslaved, so that it is not necessary to enslave their bodies. They can even be allowed to choose their governors, since they have already been taught what sort of governors they ought to choose.

It is not within the purpose of this book either to support or to refute this contention of the communists. Even if its truth is allowed, it does not follow that the poor do not consent to their governors' actions merely because they are not aware of their own best interests. They may have been deceitfully persuaded to submit themselves to laws and to social conditions which enable the rich, though only a minority, to exploit them to their own advantage. In so far as they have been deceived in this manner they have been robbed, not of the power to choose their governors, but of their prosperity and happiness. This deception is an evil, but it does not affect the question of consent. The governed consent to their governors' actions, whatever the nature of these may be, so long as they express the wish that they should be performed and so long as the expression of this wish creates the right to perform them in their governors.

It is only to the extent to which their governors deceive them into believing that they are giving effect to their wishes, though they are not in fact doing so, that the governors can truly be said to be acting without their consent in spite of the fact that they were elected to power by the governed. Propaganda in the interest of the few need not render government with the consent of the many impossible. Indeed, it is largely because it need not do so that it can truly be said to be one of the greatest evils that can affect the state.

Finally, before giving a final accurate definition of consent, and before going on to show how far under pure democratic rule, and especially under what is known as representative government, the governors can be said to rule with the consent of the governed, it is necessary to give some meaning to the word 'representative' in its political sense. If the meaning of the word 'consent' as it has been defined above is borne in mind, it is not difficult to see that one man is the representative of another only if he is his agent, i.e. only in so far as his right to perform certain actions is dependent upon the consent of the person he is said to represent.

In this connexion it must once again be admitted that the word 'representative' is not always used in the sense that has been defined. A king or a statesman is often said to be representative of a nation even when his right to act as he does depends in no way upon its consent. He is said to be representative of it when in fact his actions are such as it would approve of, or when he is supposed to possess qualities common to members of this nation in virtue of which they can be distinguished as a class of individuals from members of all other nations. In both these instances the word representative means something very different from what it means when it is said of a Member of Parliament that he is representative of the majority of his constituents. In the first instance it refers to the fact that the ruler acts habitually in ways of which his subjects approve, and in the second to the fact that he is a good specimen of the class to which they all belong. In neither case is consent implied, however true it may be, as a matter of observed fact, that men do habitually tend to choose as their agents men of whose actions they have approved in the past, or whom they consider to be *typical* of themselves.

A man in making another man his agent can give him permission either to perform certain clearly defined actions or else to promote a certain end or ends by any means which he may think necessary. In both cases the man, since his right to act depends upon permission, is equally the agent of him who gave him the permission. He may either be empowered to act for the man he represents for an unspecified period, being liable to cease to be his agent as soon as the latter should decide to take back his permission, or else for a specified period, during which the latter surrenders his right to withdraw his permission and makes himself responsible for all his agent's actions performed in his capacity as agent during the period agreed upon between them. That is to say, one man may continue to be another man's agent even if the latter should desire him to cease to be so, provided that the latter, in making him his agent, agreed that he should continue to act for him during a certain period without being liable to a withdrawal of this permission. The test is one of responsibility. If *A* empowers *B* to act for him during four years, then *A*, even if he disapproves of *B*'s actions, is also responsible for them and cannot assert that they are done without his consent. But as soon as *A* can legitimately be said to be no longer responsible for *B*'s actions, then *B* immediately ceases to be his agent. He may claim to be still acting for *A*, but he will not be doing so, either because the period agreed ·upon between them has expired or else because he is acting in matters other than those in respect of which he was made *A*'s agent.

Some people find it difficult to allow that an agent may

be empowered not only to perform certain defined actions and to pursue certain limited ends, but also to promote the general welfare of the persons he represents by any means which he may think necessary. A moment's reflection should, however, suffice to rid the mind of uneasiness on this score. The only limits set to the powers of an agent are those which define the right of the man he represents to empower him to act in his name (i.e. under such conditions that both are responsible for the former's actions). So long as the agent has been empowered to act, whatever his action, he still performs it as an agent, provided that the man who empowered him to act really had the right to do so.

One man has not the right to empower another to be his agent in respect of actions which he ought to perform himself. *A* cannot, for instance, give *B* permission to act as a husband towards his, *A*'s, wife. So also one man ought not to make himself the slave of another, bound to obey him in all things, since it would not be right for him to do so. No man can have a right to do what it is not right that he should do. *A* can, of course, obey *B* in all things and so can, in fact, make himself *B*'s slave, provided that he does obey *B* in everything. But he does not create in *B* a right to his obedience, having himself no right to grant it to him unconditionally. In the chapter on *Rights* we define a right as a power which ought to be secured to a man because its exercise is either itself good or else a means to the good. If this definition is correct it provides us with a general rule whereby we can decide whether or not one man really has a right to grant another a certain permission, and so enables us to set limits to the powers which men may grant to their agents.

It is now time to pass on to a more accurate definition of *consent*, which will be advanced as an answer to a valid objection to the loose definition already given.

To the latter it may be objected that the word 'consent' has a wider connotation than the one it offers, even when all the meanings not relevant to a discussion of representative government have been rejected. The word 'consent' is used in many meanings, and some justification must be offered of the contention that the particular meaning of it which has been selected is alone relevant to the discussion which is the subject of this book.

The objector may dislike the rigid distinction which has been made between *consent* and *approval*. He may contend that the ruler, when he does what his subjects wish because he knows them to wish it, thereby acquires a right to act as he does, and so may be said to act with their consent. If the laws which they have to obey are approved of by them, their enforcement is likely to result in less unpleasantness than might otherwise attend it. Now in a later chapter it is asserted that a man's right to exercise a power is grounded in the goodness of the exercise itself or of its consequences. If, therefore, government according to laws approved of by the governed decreases pain or increases pleasure, then (since pleasure is good and pain evil) the governors' right to act as they do is obviously, there being no other relevant considerations, increased by the fact that their actions are approved of by their subjects. We have here, then, an expression of a wish by some persons that others should act in a certain way, creating or increasing the latter's right to act in that way, and so constituting, according to the objector, a genuine case of consent.

But there is also to be considered the question of responsibility.[1] It is not sufficient for the establishment of a genuine consent that A's expression of a wish that B should act in a certain way should create or increase B's right to act in that way. Before B can be said to be acting with A's consent, in the sense of that word relevant to this present discussion, A as well as B must be responsible for B's

---

[1] Some philosophers criticize the definitions of this word offered by others, and then contend that they have proved that there is no such thing as responsibility. Such a conclusion is fallacious.

action, so that it can truly be said of the latter that he is acting with the former's permission.

Now this restriction of the meaning of the word 'consent', however little it may recommend itself to the objector, is not at all arbitrary. Government by consent is also called self-government. This latter phrase is admittedly paradoxical, and if its literal meaning is accepted must lead one to the strangest conclusions. These conclusions—of which the most famous, historically, is the absurd suggestion that it is possible to be compelled to be free—can be avoided if self-government is taken to be an elliptical phrase signifying a form of government whereby the governed can be said to be responsible for their governors' actions. The responsibility of the consenting parties and of their agents cannot, of course, be similar. If the agent is directly responsible for his action, the man whose agent he is is so only indirectly. The latter is directly responsible for making the former his agent, i.e. for giving him a certain permission.

The phrase 'indirect responsibility' is misleading. If taken literally, it is absurd. No man can possibly be responsible for another's action. But he can be responsible for enabling another man to act in a certain way, and this grant of a power is his own action, for which he is quite obviously answerable. The phrase 'indirect responsibility' will be used for the sake of convenience to express what might be expressed at greater length by the words 'responsibility for an action which grants a power or a right to another man to act in a certain way'.

A man, however, before he can be indirectly responsible for another man's action must not only act in such a way as to make it possible for the other to perform his action or in such a way as to create or increase his right to do so, but must act either with the intention of making this possible and creating this right, or else with the knowledge that he is doing so. This also applies to cases where the action creating the possibility or the right is an expression of a wish. For instance, A's expression of a wish that B should act in a certain way must not only create or increase B's right but must be known or intended by A to do so. Then, and only then, is he indirectly responsible for B's action, and his expression of a wish a genuine act of consent. A, of course, is responsible for his own action, even when he does not know that one of its consequences is to make B's action possible or to create a right in B to perform it. But he is then responsible for an action which, as a matter of fact, makes another action possible or creates a right, but not for creating the possibility or the right. A man cannot be blamed for those consequences of his actions which he neither foresaw nor intended.

In the case of A's expression of a wish that B should act in a certain way, if A had no knowledge that his action would, or intention that it should, create or increase a certain right in B, it would not amount to a permission and so would not constitute a genuine case of consent. But it might, of course, increase B's right to act as he does by giving him evidence of the fact that his doing so would please A, whose pleasure is obviously good.

Mere knowledge that his own action will make another's possible makes a man indirectly responsible for the latter's action. There is no need for him to intend that this should be so, provided only that he knows that it will. For instance, if a man through laziness or cowardice fails to perform an action which he knows will prevent a murder, he is obviously indirectly responsible for the event, though not, for that reason, a consenting party to the murderer's action. Indirect responsibility does not, therefore, imply consent. Consent, however, does imply indirect responsibility.

When the enabling action (i.e. the action performed by one man making possible another man's action or creating in him a right to perform it) is an expression of a wish, then the distinction between indirect responsibility (for what might be called the enabled action) grounded upon knowledge alone, and that grounded upon intention as well, cannot be made. For if *A* knows that his expression of a wish will enable *B* to perform a certain action, then he must also intend that it should do so. So long as his action does not merely create a power, but also a right, it is a genuine case of consent.

The definition of consent as an expression of a wish by one man that another man should act in a certain way, known and intended to create or increase in the latter the right to act in this way, may be taken as equivalent to the definition of it offered earlier in the chapter as an expression of a wish by one man that another should act in a certain way, which expression creates or increases in the latter the right so to act under such conditions that the former is also responsible for the latter's action. These definitions are both of them supposed not to be arbitrary, but to describe one of the meanings of the word 'consent' which is the only one relevant to this inquiry, since it is the only one which makes government by consent equivalent to responsible government.

If any one should object to this narrow definition of consent on the ground that approval is sometimes called consent and that its relations with political obligation are also interesting and worthy of discussion, no better reply can be made than that this book does not set out to be an inquiry into the relations which subsist between a man's duty to obey his government and every action of his which he may be inclined to call consent. The phenomenon called *consent* which is relevant to this inquiry is the only one which, in my opinion, the ordinary man would allow to be properly so called in that sense of the word which makes government by consent the same thing as responsible government. The illustrations that have been advanced have been intended not to dispute men's right to mean whatever they please by the word, but to fix the only meaning of it which is relevant to this limited inquiry. Nor can it be admitted that our equating government by consent with responsible government is at all arbitrary. Most men mean by the one phrase what they mean by the other, or, rather, the fact to which they refer is in both cases the same, though in the former one aspect of it is emphasized, whereas in the latter the emphasis is on another.

We have now offered our definition of consent and have dealt with most of the more usual abuses of the term. We have also tried to make clear what is meant by such words as 'agent' and 'representative'. It now remains to find out to what extent popular governments govern with their subjects' consent. There are only two kinds of governments that can be said to act with the consent of the majority of the governed—pure democracy and what is usually called representative democracy. Under pure democracy only those members of the government who exercise its executive and judicial functions can be said to act with the consent of the governed; those who exercise its legislative functions do not do so by consent, since their right to make laws (i.e. to vest the magistrates with the right to enforce certain rules of action) does not depend upon consent. As has been argued already, men cannot properly be said to consent to their own actions. Under representative democracy those members of the government who make the laws, as well as those who undertake its administrative and judicial functions, can be said to represent the governed in so far as their right to make laws depends upon consent.

Now that it is clear what is meant by purely democratic and by representative government, it is necessary to find out how far such governments can be said to act with the consent of the governed.

To take *pure democracy* first: it is clear that under this system only those persons who voted for a law can be said to consent to the actions of the magistrates who enforce that law. Those who voted against it cannot properly be said to consent to its enforcement, even if, in fact, they desire that it should be enforced because the majority has voted for it. A man's desire that all laws should be enforced, whether or not he has voted in favour of them, is no more than an indication that he thinks the enforcement of laws desirable; it does not carry with it consent *ex post facto* to the laws against which he voted or to those for which he did not vote at all. No doubt such a desire on the part of the great majority of the citizens of the state is indispensable if democratic government is to be possible at all. Nevertheless, the condition of the possibility of exercising power is not the same thing as the condition of the right to possess it. To say that the government could not enforce the law unless even those who voted against it desired its enforcement is not to say that the right to enforce it depends upon this desire. It is only when the desire that the government should act in a certain way is itself what gives the government the right to act in this way, so that those who express the desire are also responsible for the government's action, that the desire is also consent.

There is, however, a sense in which a man who votes against a law can also be a consenting party to its enforcement. He can be said to consent to its enforcement if the right of the majority to make laws depends upon his having agreed that any resolution should become law when the majority of citizens pronounce themselves in its favour. If, then, there existed a state the authority of whose government rested upon a unanimous agreement of all its members that any decision of the majority of them should be binding on them all, we should have a state in which all laws were consented to by every one. This unanimous consent, however, would continue only so long as all further persons, on becoming citizens, agreed to be bound by the decisions of the majority. As soon as any citizen, not having previously agreed to be bound by all majority decisions, voted against a law, the unanimity of consent to all laws would cease.

In the case of what is usually called *representative govern-*

ment it is clear that the element of consent is even more restricted than under pure democracy. There is, of course, in this case legislation, as well as administration, by consent, but whereas under pure democracy there is in each case of the making of a law a special consent on the part of the majority of the people that the law should be enforced, under representative government what the majority of the people consent to directly is rather the making of laws by certain persons than the enforcement of specific laws.

Again, under *representative democracy* the actual consent to the laws made is much more likely than under pure democracy to be the consent of a minority of the people, even where, in both cases, the whole adult population habitually votes either for the laws or for the law-makers, as the case may be. Under the present British electoral system it is not always certain that the members of the Lower House do represent a majority of the voters. It may be that the number of votes cast for successful candidates in any particular election is less than the number of votes cast for unsuccessful candidates, especially when there have been many three-cornered elections. But even if, in fact, the House of Commons does usually represent the majority of the people who troubled to vote, it does not necessarily represent more than a bare majority of them. All the members of the House, taken together, may represent a majority of the adult population, if indeed the whole of this population actually voted, but even then a majority of the House need not represent a majority of the people and is, in fact, actually more likely to represent a minority. It follows, therefore, that the vast majority of the laws of this country have been consented to by only a minority of the people. *Proportional representation* would, however, ensure that the legislature was representative not merely of a majority of the voters but of so large a majority that any majority of the House was likely to be representative of a majority of the people. A good system of proportional representation would in all probability make representative government just as much government by consent as pure democracy. Consent would be in some cases more indirect, but it would, of course, be just as much consent. The permission of A given to B to give permission to C to do something is just as much a permission given by A to C as if B had not existed at all.

The task of estimating how far, for instance, modern British governments rule with the consent of their subjects is further complicated by the altered significance of the general election. In the eighteenth century the electors chose representatives not to carry out certain specified ends but to promote the welfare of the nation, or, rather, to rule it, using any means which they thought fit. But in modern times the majority, or relative majority, of the members of the House of Commons are pledged to put through a certain legislative programme, and they are not supposed to have the moral right to refuse to do so. The executive which is chosen from their number is expected to see to it that electoral promises are honoured. It is also expected, by some at least of its subjects, not to introduce other important legislative proposals without first awaiting the verdict of the nation at a general election. Other persons, on the other hand, maintain that though the government is pledged to put through certain legislative proposals, it is also free to introduce any other measures it may think fit, since it has a mandate not only to make certain specified laws but also to promote the general welfare by any means it judges to be necessary.

Now when it is not known exactly what the electors desire their representatives to do, it is not possible to estimate the extent to which the government acts with the consent of its subjects. The nature of the mandate must always be defined, however limited or however wide it may be. It need not, of course, be defined by law, but merely by custom and tradition, so that the elector, at least, knows what he is doing.

The fact that the legislative programmes submitted to the electorate are drawn up in the central offices of the various parties does not hamper, but, on the contrary, makes possible, government by consent. It is not the persons who choose the programmes but those who choose between them who decide what laws are to be added to the Statute Book. The party system, for all its faults, alone makes it possible to find out how the majority of the people wishes to be governed. The fact that the parties are more skilful in putting desires into the minds of the people than they are in giving effect to them does not make the desires any the less desires. Indeed, the leaders of a party, if they are honest men sincerely interested in promoting the welfare of their fellow countrymen, will be as earnest in their attempt to stimulate the right desires amongst the electorate as to give effect to them should they be called upon to do so. If they do not do this they will leave the field open to others less scrupulous than themselves who, by making representative government a mockery, will prepare the ground for one of the new-fangled tyrannies which, unlike the older ones, are not content merely to misgovern but must also pervert their subjects. What is needed is not the rule of the people by the people, which is impossible even under pure democracy, since magistrates must necessarily be fewer than their subjects, but the rule of the people by their betters with the consent of as many of them as possible.

We see, then, that both under pure democracy and under representative democracy there is no such thing as government by the consent of all the persons supposed to owe obedience to the government. Under the very best possible conditions, so far as consent is concerned, it may be true that the rights of the governors depend upon the consent of a majority of the governed, but never upon the consent of all persons who can rightly be said to be obliged to obey the law. It follows from this that consent cannot be taken to be the only basis of political obligation.

But to say that consent is not the only basis of political obligation is not to say that it is not, when given, a basis of obligation. It may be true that the most important basis of political obligation is not consent; it may also be true that a man may at times be morally obliged to disobey a law to the enforcement of which he has consented in the past; but it does not follow that the fact of having consented to it in the past does not, other considerations apart, create a further obligation to obey it. In fact it is quite clear that consent does impose a special obligation of this kind upon the consenting party.

Moreover, it may further be true that a man is, *ceteris paribus*, under an obligation to obey a law because the majority of his fellows consented to its enforcement. Whether any such obligation does exist is more open to doubt, perhaps, than the existence of the obligation mentioned in the previous paragraph. However that may be, its non-existence cannot be inferred from the fact that the man in question did not consent to the law.

Nor does it follow, because to live under the protection of a certain government and under the protection of certain laws does not constitute consent to the existence of that government and those laws, that it does not impose upon the protected person an obligation to obey them. The obligation, in this instance, would not arise out of consent, but would be no more than a special case of the general obligation to help persons who benefit us. Locke and Rousseau were perfectly right when they insisted that protection by the law creates an obligation to obey the law, but they were wrong in maintaining that the acceptance of protection by the law implies consent to its enforcement.

Lastly it may be true that government with the consent of the governed is the best form humanly possible. If this, indeed, is the case, then the obligation to obey such a government is stronger than the obligation to obey any other form of government, not merely because it is based upon consent to the greatest extent possible, but because its being so based is the condition of the existence of other things which every rational being is obliged to promote.

CHAPTER II
THE GENERAL WILL

IN the last chapter we gave our definition of *consent* and criticized some of the more usual abuses of the term. But we did not consider the doctrine of the existence of a *general* or *real will*, which is, after all, primarily a theory of the nature of consent. That it is so is evident in the political writings of its originator, J.-J. Rousseau, and also in those of its nineteenth-century elaborators, who insisted that it was intended to show that the subjects of the state were perfectly free even when they appeared to be coerced. It would, for instance, never have been necessary for Bosanquet to worry himself over the paradox of self-government had he not thought that consent ought to be the only basis of political obligation.

But before we go on to explain and criticize this doctrine at some length we will try to show how it arose as an attempt to overcome the more glaring deficiencies in the theory of the contract philosophers. These latter, as is well known, soon found themselves in great difficulties as a result of their endeavour to prove consent to be the sole basis of political obligation. They saw that the vast majority of persons obeying some sovereign authority or other had never explicitly consented to do so, but they were unwilling to admit that upon their theory these persons were under no obligation to obey their rulers. On the other hand, they were unwilling to admit that their theory was false. They therefore expanded the meaning of the word 'consent' so that it should be taken to cover all sorts of other facts which did not partake of the nature of consent at all but which could fairly plausibly be supposed to be in some way connected with the obligation to obey the government. It was clear to them, for instance, that to receive benefits creates obligations towards the providers of them on the part of the persons who receive them. They saw that to be protected by the law creates, on the part of the person protected, an obligation to obey the law. They therefore tried to make out that to accept the protection of the law was equivalent to a tacit consent to the general governmental activities of the persons who enforced the law, and that here also there was a case of an obligation to obey the government ultimately based upon consent.

Now it was not long before philosophers became dissatisfied with these rather crude endeavours to maintain the contract theory through a distortion of the proper meaning of the word 'consent'. They saw that it was no use giving the name 'consent' to what was not properly *consent* at all. They therefore altered their method of approach and tried to make out that, as a matter of fact, the governed always do consent to the actions of their governors, even if they appear not to be doing so. Rousseau is the first of the modern philosophers who took up this line of argument, although he did so only tentatively and in fact retained many of the more important elements of the contract theories of his predecessors. It was not until Hegel wrote his *Philosophy of Right* that the old contract theory was finally abandoned and that a new explanation of why it is a man's duty to obey the government was offered in its stead.

This new explanation did not really reject the thesis that consent is the sole basis of political obligation, but it attempted to interpret it in such a way as to avoid the difficulties which had ruined the contract theory. Instead of attempting to prove that consent was involved in facts which quite obviously did not involve it, it attempted to show that there existed so close a relation between the will of the governed and that of their governors, in so far as it was *expressed* in the law, that any real conflict between them was impossible. The governed, according to this explanation, always wanted to do what the law required them to do, even when, in fact, they might appear not to want to do so.

Moreover, they wanted to act in this way, not because the law required that they should do so, but because what they really wanted to do was in every case precisely what the law enjoined.

We see, then, that philosophers have attempted to reinstate consent as the sole basis of political obligation, on the plea that the law gives effect to a social will, which is, at the same time, the *real will* of the governed, so that the obligation to obey the law derives from the fact that the law gives effect to this real will. We must obey the government—the interpreter of the *social will*—because it is really doing nothing other than enforcing our will. We are therefore always consenting parties to its actions, even if we are not conscious of being so. All government, in so far as it enforces the law, is, according to this theory, necessarily representative government.

It is very difficult to see how this peculiar theory can allow of consent at all in the definition of it which was given in the last chapter. For it was there said that no man could, properly speaking, consent to his own actions, whereas this theory urges us to believe that a man is always a consenting party to all the actions of the government, on the ground that they are, in the last analysis, his own actions. To the extent to which this theory denies the real numerical difference between the wills of all the members of the State, whether they are governors or governed, it makes consent both impossible and unnecessary. It would also appear that this theory makes not only consent impossible and unnecessary but also political obligation. If the state always does what the individual wishes, for the reason that both their wills are really the same will, there is no need for an explanation of how it is the duty of the subject to obey the government even when it requires him to do what he does not wish. None the less, since the inventors of this theory suppose that it is a theory of consent and political obligation, it is obvious that we are bound to consider it.

The four thinkers whose theories of the *social will* we will treat of here are Rousseau, Hegel, Bosanquet, and Green. There are certain elements common to them all, but, all things considered, the theories of Hegel and Bosanquet are the most alike, though important similarities exist between those of Green and Rousseau.

Hegel and Bosanquet insist chiefly upon the existence of a *rational* or *social will*. They assert that the existence of this will and its *expression* in the institutions and activities of the state is the common good of the citizens. Rousseau and Green, on the other hand, tend to think of the general will as *general* only in so far as it has for its object a common good. It is true that Rousseau often means even less than this and makes no distinction at all between the general will and the will of the majority, but in so far as he does not do so we are not interested in his theory. We are interested in it only to the extent to which it can fairly be said to postulate the existence of a social will.

We will deal first of all with the *general will* as it appears in the writings of Rousseau and Green, and then, when we have done this, we shall be able to go on to a consideration of the much more complicated conception of the *real will* as it was elaborated by Hegel in his *Philosophy of Right* and explained in England by Bosanquet in his *Philosophical Theory of the State*.

To begin, then, with Rousseau and Green: if we take two typical definitions of the general will from these two authors, we shall see in both cases the emphasis laid upon the community of the good which is the object of the social will. The argument is essentially from the common good to the social will. Indeed, Rousseau rarely, and Green never, states that the social will is a single distinct will. Its unity, both imply, lies rather in the unity of its object than in that of the social being whose will it is supposed to be. 'There is often a great deal of difference between the will of all and the general will; the latter regards only the common interest, while the former has regard to private interests, and is merely a sum of particular wills; but take away from these same wills the pluses and minuses which cancel one another, and the general will remains as the sum of the differences.'[1] Here Rousseau distinctly defines the *general will* as the will which has for its object the common good. In fact its existence depends upon the promotion of the common good, for if the wills of the citizens do not offset each other in such a way as to allow of the promotion of the common good, the general will simply does not exist.

Green defines the *general will* as 'that impalpable congeries of the hopes and fears of a people, bound together by common interests and sympathy'.[2] Here the general will is not really an individual will at all. It is no more than the sum of all the wishes of the individuals who form a community, in so far as they have common objects and are determined by unselfish motives. This mere *congeries* hardly deserves the name used by the thinkers we are considering. What is asserted to be general is the object of many individual wills, and not the wills themselves, for Green always supposed them to be merely particular.

Rousseau and Green both speak as though the existence of a common good implied the existence of a common will, but when called upon to state exactly what this common will is they call it no more than the sum of individual wills in so far as their effects tend to the common good. Rousseau sets the greater emphasis upon the singleness of the will which wills the common good, whereas Green never explicitly allows that it is single, though both often write as if the singleness of the will followed from the singleness of its object. In fact, if they did not imply at least this much they would have no right to talk of a general will at all. As it is, whenever they make it clear what they think the general will is, its general character tends to disappear.

---

[1] *Contrat Social*, Book II, chap. iii, p. 1.
[2] T. H. Green, *Lectures on Political Obligation* (London, 1924), p. 98.

They treat it as an individual existent only when the context is such that they do not need to state but need only imply its character. Rousseau is much the less consistent of the two. On occasions he speaks of the *general will* as though its generality consisted merely in the fact that it is the will of a majority, at other times as if its generality consisted in its being the faculty of a super-mind. He talks of a common self and a public person, and of the State as of something which has mental and moral attributes of its own. To the extent to which he does this his theory is more closely akin to that of Hegel and Bosanquet, and it will therefore be dealt with when we discuss the theories of the two latter. Nevertheless, it is rather in his resemblances with Green than in those with Hegel that we find the main contention of Rousseau as regards the nature of the general will.

The bare statement of the contention immediately reveals the fallacy upon which it is grounded. There is simply no argument from the existence of a good common to several people to a will which is also common to them.[1] Indeed, the fact that there is no such argument is made evident by what happens whenever Rousseau and Green try to give an accurate definition of the general will. As we have already pointed out, they always lose sight of its singleness and speak of it as if it were merely the sum of individual wills in so far as their interaction tends to cause the existence of a certain effect. They talk of it as of a mere multiplicity of wills which gain a new common characteristic over and above the common characteristics of all wills as such, owing to the fact that they are all supposed to be part-causes of one and the same effect. The general will thus becomes the class of all wishes which have for their object a common good to be shared by all the subjects of the wishes. It is not properly a will at all. And yet, as has been said already,

---

[1] The fact that the existence of a common good is itself doubtful is not brought into the argument at this stage. It will be fully dealt with in the next chapter.

both these thinkers, except when they are actually defining it, talk of the general will as if it were a real individual will, although Green, at least, never explicitly calls it one and never mentions any public person to whom it might belong.

The fallacy implied by the Rousseau-Green doctrine of the general will is not one to which philosophers alone are liable. Most of the elaborate mistakes made by political thinkers, especially by Rousseau and the Idealists of the next century, are implicit in ordinary speech. It is probable that men co-operating to realize common ends have always been in the habit of using metaphorical language which, if taken literally, suggested that they regarded themselves as having only one will between them. So also men who did not presume to call themselves philosophers spoke of the nation to which they belonged as if it were a single person with passions, prejudices, and ambitions exactly similar to their own. These ordinary metaphors, clothed in new and extraordinary language, were changed into philosophical theories and hailed as profound and original discoveries.

We must now pass on to a consideration of the doctrine of the *real will* as we find it in the writings of Hegel and Bosanquet. These thinkers regard the individual as, from the first, no more than a partial and incomplete 'expression' of something greater than himself. This greater something is in reality a super-ego, and the *general* or *real will* belongs essentially to it. This super-ego is the State, and it is a *fuller* and more complete being than any individual can possibly be. It is not denied that states can be evil, but this possibility does not destroy the theory. Man can be evil, but the fact of his evil character does not prevent his being a *higher* type than the most developed animal. 'Evil behaviour can doubtless disfigure it in many ways, but the ugliest man, the criminal, the invalid, the cripple are living men. The positive thing, the life, is present in spite of defects, and it is with this affirmative that we have to deal.'[1]

[1] Hegel's *Philosophy of Right*, translated by W. Wallace, p. 247.

To get at the essence of Hegel's notion of the State it is best to quote some passages from his *Philosophy of Right*. 'The State', he says, 'is the realized ethical idea or ethical spirit' . . . 'The State is absolutely rational.' . . . '[Its] substantive unity is its . . . absolute end.'[1] That is to say, the State is its own end. There is not a common good which is not necessarily attained by the State, but which ought to be its end, as with Rousseau and Green. The good which is common to all the members of the State is the existence of the State of which they are members. Thus the end of the State—its own existence—'has the highest right over the individual whose highest duty in turn is to be a member of the State'. . . . 'It [the State] is the objective spirit, and he [the individual] has his truth, real existence, and ethical status only in being a member of it.'[2]

Bosanquet takes practically the same view of the nature of the State, although the necessity of dealing with critics, who could not attack Hegel during his lifetime, makes him to a certain extent more cautious and less dogmatic in his statements. It is from him rather than from Hegel that we get a detailed account of the relation between the individual and the State, and an explanation of just how it is that the individual becomes a moral being only in so far as he is a member of a state. It is because he had to deal with utilitarian and sociological critics who did not worry Hegel that his account is much more complete and a good deal easier to understand. It would not, however, be fair to Hegel to suppose, because his account of the nature of the relation between the individual and the State is less full and carefully thought out than Bosanquet's, that 'he ignored the importance of the individual'. Nothing can be more shortsighted than a criticism of Hegel on the ground that he advocated the entire subordination of the individual to the State. In one sense he did advocate it, but not exactly in the

---

[1] Ibid., p. 240.
[2] Ibid.

sense of his adversaries. The entire subordination of the individual to the State involved, in his opinion, the highest development of the individual's own best characteristics. 'The modern State has enormous strength and depth, in that it allows the principle of subjectivity to complete itself to an independent extreme of personal peculiarity, and yet at the same time brings it back to the substantive unity, and thus preserves particularity in the principle of the State.'[1] 'The universal must be actively furthered, but, on the other side, subjectivity must be wholly and vitally developed. Only when both elements are present in force is the State to be regarded as articulate and truly organised. . . . the State is . . . strong in its union of the universal with the particular interests of individuals. Thus just so far as people have duties to fulfil towards it, they have also rights.'[2] Here we see that the existence of the State, as the *articulation* of an ethical idea, is just as much dependent upon the moral development and freedom of its members as these latter are on the existence of the State. 'It has often been said that the end of the State is the happiness of the citizens. This is indeed true.'[3]

Nevertheless, it is from Bosanquet that we get the more complete account of the relation of the individual to the State, and of the ordinary individual will to the social will. We will therefore, in criticizing the Idealist theory, consider it chiefly as it is elucidated by Bosanquet. First of all it will be necessary to give a general account of the theory as it appears in Bosanquet's *Philosophical Theory of the State*.

Bosanquet begins with what he calls the paradox of self-government. How can the self be self-governing when suffering social coercion? At first sight it appears that all government must necessarily be coercive and that all use of force by the state is *ipso facto* a restriction of the freedom of

---

[1] Hegel's *Philosophy of Right*, p. 248.
[2] Ibid., p. 249.   [3] Ibid., p. 254.

the individual. And yet it is supposed that the State should in some way give effect to the will of the governed. If it does not do this, it is ordinarily supposed to have less value than if it does. But, as Bosanquet saw, and as has been pointed out in the last chapter, mere external consent cannot go far. The very fact that a law must often be maintained by force shows that it does not always give effect to the actual wishes of the governed. Indeed, whenever the law is enforced and not just habitually obeyed, it is enforced contrary to the wish of the individual against whom it is applied. Bosanquet agrees that there is one sense of the word 'freedom' which makes the phrase 'forced to be free' a mere contradiction in terms.

In place of the old doctrine of *external* or *explicit* consent, Bosanquet tries to provide a more adequate doctrine of *internal* or *implicit* consent. This *consent* is not implicit in the sense that it is a wish which can be reasonably inferred from the individual's present action or abstinence from action. Such *consent*, if indeed it can exist, Bosanquet would regard as just as external as ordinary explicit consent. The more adequate doctrine of consent must go hand in hand with a more adequate account of freedom. If we can intelligibly be said to consent to being forced to do something against our present wish, there must be some kind of freedom which will make it possible for us to do what we wish to do when we appear to be forced to do the direct contrary. This kind of freedom, which provides the solution of the initial paradox, Bosanquet regards as positive, in distinction from the merely negative freedom which is freedom from external constraint.

This positive freedom involves not only freedom from external constraint but freedom from constraint by the lower emotions and impulses which belong to man in his non-rational character. It follows, therefore, that man is free to the extent to which his will is determined by reason. To act rationally is to act freely: to act irrationally is to be

constrained by one's lower nature. The will in so far as it is
determined by reason Bosanquet calls the *real* or *good will*,
and in so far as it is determined by non-rational impulses,
the *actual* will. The real will is good, because it can only
find permanent satisfaction in ends determined for it by
reason; and, for Bosanquet, satisfactoriness and goodness
are the same thing. He justifies this apparently unjustified
use of the word 'real' by an appeal to the ordinary use of the
word 'self-control'. A man is said to control himself when
his will is determined by reason, and he is also often said
not to be 'himself' when his will is controlled by non-
rational impulses. Ordinary language, therefore, does seem
to imply that a man is himself when he is what he ought to
be, and that what he ought to be is a rational creature.
There seems, then, to Bosanquet to be an important distinction between the *real* and the *actual*. But the distinction
is not exactly what might be expected at first sight. The
actual is not all that exists and the *real* merely that part of it
which is what it ought to be. The real is what ought to
exist and also what really does exist, whereas the actual is
merely what appears to exist. So that the *real* self, the *good*
self, the *rational* self, and the *free* self are identical.

Now when the state coerces the individual in the name of
the law, it is forcing his actual self to do what his real self
wishes to do. It is therefore forcing him to be free. It
might be asked at this stage, even if the validity of the distinction between the real and the actual self is not ques-
tioned, what guarantee there is that what the state forces the
individual's actual self to do is precisely what his real self
wishes to do. Bosanquet's reply is that the general will and
the individual's real will are identical and that the state is
the interpreter and enforcer of the general will.

Bosanquet does not at first go so far as to assert that the
state is a single social active mind. He calls it 'The operative criticism of all institutions—the modification and ad-
justment by which they are capable of playing a rational

part in the object of human will'.[1] The state is rather the embodiment of rational wishes and rational thoughts, systematized into law and enforced upon individuals by the persons entrusted with the government. It is not merely the law, still less the actual imponents of the law, but rather law as a system of interferences with the individual which tend to make him more and more what he ought to be and therefore, at the same time, what he really is. The state is thus, in Hegel's words, *objective mind*. The *general will* is the rational will embodied in law. It can, therefore, in Hegelian phraseology, be called *objective will*. As operative in the lives of ordinary individuals it is the State. It is not denied that all laws have been made by individuals, but it is asserted that the law, as a system of rules, is much more the product of reason than are the wishes of any ordinary individual. It is the fruit of the reasoning of many individuals embodied in a coherent system of rules which, if obeyed, tend to make the persons who obey them better than they were before.

The phrase 'objective mind' has, however, both for Hegel and for Bosanquet, a more important meaning than just the rational wishes of many individuals expressed in a system of law. There is, over and above the law, an idea which finds *articulation* in it. The general will is not therefore merely the law as the embodiment of the past and present rational wishes of actual individuals. It is itself something quite distinct from the wills of individuals, although it only finds expression through them. That is to say, it is not fully understood if it is thought of as a will merely metaphorically, in the sense of a code of laws made by many wills and enforced with the approval of many wills. For then it would be no more than the effect of numerous and private, though harmonious and rational, wishes. It would not be a will at all, but merely the effect of many past willings.

[1] *Philosophical Theory of the State*, p. 151.

The real will of individuals, their will as determined by reason, expresses itself whenever men by common agreement make good laws. But this real will is not, says Bosanquet, ultimately an individual will at all. It is the general or social will expressing itself through the individual. So that there exists a will, over and above the actual wills of individuals, which is the real will of all the members of the State. It is not merely that individual wills, in so far as they are determined by reason, are similar and that there is a qualitative identity particularized in them. The real will of one individual has not merely precisely identical ends with the real wills of all other individuals; it is, at the same time, their real wills. The identity referred to here is not qualitative but numerical. There is definitely alleged to be a real or general will which is the will of society and, at the same time, the will of all individuals in so far as they are determined to action by reason.

Bosanquet takes the reality of the individual to be not what at any time he actually appears to be, but rather what he ought to be. But in so far as he is what he ought to be his will ceases to be merely his own and becomes simultaneously the will of all other persons in so far as they are what they ought to be. From this it might seem to follow that the separateness of the individual is mere appearance, and that the reality is the idea which, as the general or real will, finds expression in the law. The isolation of the individual both Hegel and Bosanquet would assert to be in the last analysis mere illusion. But the difference of one individual from another they would consider to be very far from illusion. The very nature of the general will is to 'manifest' itself through the wills of ordinary individuals. Its identity consists in their difference. Thus, as a final explanation of the nature of the relation between the State and the individual both Hegel and Bosanquet offer the fundamental category of Idealist philosophy—the Concrete Universal.

Bosanquet's general theory may be summed up in the following propositions. (1) Self-government alone is compatible with the moral dignity of the individual. (2) It is therefore necessary to reconcile this self-government with his apparent subjection to other persons' wills whenever he is forced to obey the laws of the State. (3) This reconciliation of incompatibles, however impossible it may seem at first sight, can be effected as soon as a proper distinction is made between positive and negative freedom. (4) Positive freedom requires the absence of restraint by one's lower impulses, and consists in the motivation of the will by rational desires. (5) In so far as the will is motivated by such desires it may be called *real* and *good*, but in so far as it is motivated by the lower, evil, and irrational impulses it is not really a will at all, but merely appears to be one. (6) The *real will* of one individual is numerically identical with the real wills of all other individuals and is the same thing as the *general will*, which is an identity manifesting itself in difference and existing only as so manifested. (7) This *general will* is expressed in the law, so that it follows that the individual, when he appears to be forced to obey the law against his apparent wish, is really being forced to do what he wishes, and is thus a consenting party to all enforcements of the law.

In our criticism of Bosanquet it will be unnecessary for us to consider the first two of the seven propositions in which we have attempted to summarize his general theory, since they are the statement of his problem rather than his solution of it. We will therefore begin by taking the third, fourth, and fifth propositions and considering them together, since none of them is intelligible if taken separately.

The *real*, the rational, the good, and the free will are, according to Bosanquet, numerically identical. But this does not mean that reality is the same thing as rationality or goodness or freedom. It means only that reality is necessarily connected with rationality, goodness, and freedom.

Nothing can possess one of these four qualities without, at the same time, possessing the three others.

Our task, then, is to find out whether any such necessary connexions exist. If we find that they do not, then it will follow that the fourth and fifth propositions, whose truth depends upon their existence, will be false and that the distinction referred to in the third proposition will be no proper distinction at all.

It will not be necessary to consider each and every alleged necessary connexion, but to take only one of them, since the existence of any one of them implies, according to Bosanquet, the existence of all the others. For instance, if we were to ask him why only the real will is good, his answer would largely turn on the assertion that it alone is rational. We will therefore confine ourselves to the consideration of the alleged connexion which can be expressed in the proposition 'only the good is real'. We will attempt to find out exactly what Bosanquet means by the words 'reality' and 'goodness', and then go on to show that reality cannot possibly mean what he supposes, and that therefore the necessary connexion he speaks of cannot exist. An explanation will also be offered of the everyday confusion between reality and goodness, which lends a certain plausibility to the Idealist assertion of a necessary connexion between them. When this has been done there will follow a criticism of the distinction between positive and negative freedom and also of the very vague use made of the word 'will' by Hegelians, which explains how it is possible for them to arrive at some of the startling conclusions in which they delight. The third, fourth, and fifth propositions will, by that time, have been refuted to the best of our ability, and it will only remain for us to consider the sixth and seventh.

Before we consider the statement 'only the good is real' (which we must suppose to be acceptable to Bosanquet, since he tells us that our true self is our self as it ought to be and, therefore, is) we must find out whether Hobhouse's criticism of him, to the effect that he confuses goodness and reality, is justified. It appears that it is not, for Bosanquet's definitions of reality and goodness in his *Principles of Individuality and Value* show quite definitely that he did not suppose them to be identical. Hobhouse's criticism misses the point. It is undeniable, of course, that Bosanquet often means by the words 'real' and 'good' something other than most people mean by them. But it does not follow from this that he takes the two words to be synonymous. He might, for instance, consider the statement 'only the good is real' to be true, but he would not consider it to be identical. When he says that something is real he does not think that he is also saying that it is good, although he might think that its goodness followed from its reality. 'Man', he might say, 'is real only in so far as he is what he ought to be', but apparently man is so not because reality and goodness are one and the same thing, but because only the good is real. Bosanquet does not confuse goodness and reality, but he claims that there is a necessary connexion between them.

In order to test the validity of this claim it is necessary, so far as it is possible to do so, to find out exactly what it is that Bosanquet means by the words 'real' and 'good'. To take the first word first: it is clear at once that Bosanquet means by the word 'real' at least as much as every one means by it when the word is being used in its proper meaning. When he says that something is real, he means at least that it exists. It is not merely that he thinks that a thing's being real entails its existence. He agrees that existence is necessarily part of the meaning of the word 'reality', but unfortunately he does not think that it constitutes its whole meaning.

The reason that he advances for not simply equating reality and existence is that, according to him, mere existence by itself is unthinkable. 'What is,' he asserts, 'is by determinate self-maintenance. There is no meaning in "it is" apart from "it is what it is".[1] It is difficult to attach any meaning to his phrase 'determinate self-maintenance'. At different times he describes it as 'that which must stand; that which has nothing without to set against it',[2] and alternatively that which is 'not self-contradictory' and possesses 'logical stability'.[3] He tells us what it is that possesses all these properties, and he implies that it could not exist unless it possessed them. It seems, therefore, that when he says that a thing is real he is saying not only that it exists but also that it possesses certain properties which, he thinks, it must possess if it is to be possible for it to exist at all. We are, then, to understand by the word 'reality' both existence and the necessary conditions of existence.

Now, it is clear that Bosanquet assumes that anything which possesses these properties, which he takes to be part of the meaning of the word 'real', also possesses the property of being good. He does not, however, suppose that any one of these properties is what is meant by the word 'good'. And yet unless he does make this supposition it is clear that there is no sense in which he can be said to confuse *goodness* and *reality*. He tells us that 'What in this sense [in the sense of being logically stable] is more real, that is more at one with itself and the whole [e.g. free from contradiction], is also the experience in which the mind obtains the more durable and coherent satisfaction, and more completely realizes itself.[4] This consideration prescribes the nature of the ultimate good or end, which is the supreme standard of value and cannot itself be measured by anything else.' 'Degrees of logical stability, of reality, are the standard by which satisfactoriness, worth and the character of being an ultimate end, are to be measured.'[5]

---

[1] Bosanquet, *Principles of Individuality and Value*, p. 44.
[2] Ibid., p. 68.
[3] Ibid., p. 46. We see the connexion in Bosanquet's mind between the real and the rational.
[4] These expressions illustrate the connexion between the rational and the good as it appeared to Bosanquet.
[5] Ibid., p. 299.

'Value', he tells us, in capital letters at the top of a page, 'is the power to satisfy.'[1] It would seem, then, that Bosanquet means by 'good' exactly what Green meant by it. 'Goodness' and 'satisfactoriness' they both take to be one and the same thing. They do not, however, equate the property of being satisfactory with the property of being 'apparently' desired. Men often appear to desire what, in fact, does not satisfy them. Bosanquet maintains that only those things which possess the properties which are conditions of the possibility of existence do, in fact, possess the property of being able to give satisfaction. If this is true, and if all the other assertions he has made about 'reality' are also true, it necessarily follows that all things which exist are good.

Bosanquet, however, goes further than this; he goes on to assert that, though men often appear to desire what does not satisfy them, these desires are, in the last resort, illusory. Men do not really desire what does not satisfy them, so that what they really desire and what really satisfies them are one and the same thing. He does not, however, equate *goodness* and *desiredness*, and therefore does not equate *satisfactoriness* and *desiredness*. Exactly the same things possess the properties of being real, of being satisfactory, and of being· desired. Nevertheless, Bosanquet regards these properties as quite separable in thought, however inseparable in fact.

The first of Bosanquet's contentions that we must discuss is that which asserts that mere existence by itself is unthinkable. 'There is no meaning in "it is" apart from "it is what it is".' It is quite clear that all things which exist possess properties of some kind or other. Otherwise, of course, there would be nothing whose existence could be asserted. It is obvious that a thing which has no properties cannot exist, for to have no properties is to be nothing, and mere nothing cannot exist. But it does not follow from this that to exist and to possess certain properties is one and the

---

[1] Ibid., p. 297; cf. *Philosophical Theory of the State*, p. 182.

same thing. Existence, as Kant pointed out, is not a property which a thing can be said to possess at all. When it is said that a thing is *real*, it is not said of it that, over and above all other properties which it possesses, it also possesses the property of being real, but merely that it, along with all its properties, does, in fact, exist. Moore suggests that the conception of reality as a property which things can possess is due to the form of language which enables us to say 'this thing is real', as if our assertion were of the same kind as the assertion 'this thing is green', whereas what we are saying in the first assertion is 'this thing exists' and in the second 'this thing possesses the quality of greenness'.[1] Bosanquet, of course, sees quite clearly that when we say that a thing exists we are not adding anything to our knowledge of its nature, that is to say we are not saying anything about it which can enter into the widest possible catalogue of its properties. And he thinks that if we are not doing this we are really not saying anything about it at all. On the other hand, he will have it that when we say that a thing is real we are in fact adding to our knowledge of its nature. He thinks, therefore, that we must mean more when we say that a thing is real than merely that it exists.

It is not difficult to see wherein Bosanquet's mistake lies. He has no right to assume that all propositions in the form '*A* is *B*' can be significant only if they definitely assert of *A* that it possesses the property *B*. The proposition '*A* is real', being identical with the proposition '*A* exists', cannot assert of *A* that it possesses any property whatever, and yet it obviously does assert something of *A*, and is therefore significant.

But, even if Bosanquet is quite wrong in asserting that existence is only part of the meaning of the word 'reality', it may yet be true that all things which exist possess the properties which he takes to be the *sine quibus non* of existence,

[1] See 'The Conception of Reality', by G. E. Moore, in *Philosophical Studies* (London, 1922).

and that only things possessing these properties and no others are capable of satisfying desire. That is to say, it may still be true that only the real is good.

All things which exist, says Bosanquet, must not be self-contradictory, and they must form part of a coherent whole. That is to say, they must not possess incompatible properties, and they must not be such that their existence is incompatible with the existence of other things which exist. If this were all that he meant by such phrases as 'logical stability', 'self-maintenance', and 'at one with itself', there would be no denying that these properties are necessary to all existing things, although it might then be urged that many things possessing them would not be likely to satisfy nor yet to be desired. Bosanquet, however, means much more than this. The *coherence* and the *non-contradiction* to which he refers involve much closer relations between the things which cohere than mere logical compatibility and mere external side-by-sideness. The things which cohere must be so related to one another that they can exist only because they are all manifestations of one and the same spiritual unity, which exists only in so far as it is *manifested* in them. This spiritual unity is the Absolute, which is, according to Bosanquet, the only thing which ultimately exists. The Absolute he takes to be an *individual*, but he does not, in this connexion, mean only what is ordinarily meant by that word. He also takes it to be a *universal*, but once again he attaches a special further meaning to his words. The Absolute, which is at once an individual and a universal, is such that it is nothing apart from its parts and also such that its parts are nothing apart from it. This last phrase, if it is to have any meaning at all, must mean at least that the parts which compose the Absolute possess only relational properties, for if they possessed other properties as well it would be impossible for them to be nothing apart from the whole.

Now it is quite clear that nothing can exist if all the

properties which it possesses are such that it could not possess them unless it formed part of something greater than itself. All things which possess relational properties must also possess properties which are not relational, for if they did not possess these latter properties they would be nothing, and therefore could not be related to anything. So far, then, from being necessary conditions of existence, the properties which Bosanquet ascribes to all real things are precisely such that no real things could possibly possess them.

If, then, nothing could possibly possess the peculiar properties which Bosanquet ascribes to all existing things as necessary conditions of their existence, it follows either that none of the things which have the power of satisfying desire can possibly exist, or else that if any such things do exist they do not possess any of the properties which, according to Bosanquet, a thing must possess before it can satisfy desire. For, if it is true that nothing can satisfy desire unless it possesses these properties, then, since there is nothing that possesses these properties, nothing can satisfy desire. On the other hand, if there actually do exist things which can satisfy desire, it follows that all things which satisfy desire need not possess these properties. That is to say, it follows either that there are no good things in the universe, or else that, if there are any, they do not possess the properties of 'coherence' and 'logical stability'. In either case it is quite clear that there is no necessary connexion between reality and goodness. If, then, we perceive that a certain thing is not good, we cannot infer that it does not exist and that its apparent existence is mere illusion. For instance, it is not possible to conclude that a bad motive for action, merely because it is bad, is not properly a motive for action at all.

Since, for the purposes of this argument, we are interested only in Bosanquet's beliefs about reality and about the peculiar connexion which he supposes to exist between reality and goodness, it is not necessary to pay special

attention to what he has to say about goodness itself. He
equates it with satisfactoriness and thus becomes guilty
of what Moore calls the naturalistic fallacy. It should, however, be noted that Bosanquet had read Moore's *Principia
Ethica* at the time when he gave his lectures on 'The Principles of Individuality and Value', and apparently was not
convinced by the arguments therein contained against views
such as his own.

Many persons besides Bosanquet have believed that there
exists some special relation between reality and goodness,
though doubtless they would not all have insisted that every
existing thing is necessarily good. They would rather have
urged that only good things can exist for long, on the ground
that what is evil tends to destroy itself. Some of them, of
course, would have gone as far as Bosanquet and would
have asserted that evil cannot possibly exist. This being so,
it would not be out of place to attempt to show how the
opinion that good tends to perpetuate itself and evil to destroy itself develops into the opinion that only the good
really exists, and that the existence of evil is, in the last
resort, *illusory*. In the first book of the *Republic* Socrates
proves to Thrasymachus that justice is more profitable than
injustice. The common saying has it that 'honesty is the
best policy'. There is, in fact, a strong consensus of opinion
in favour of the view that the good life leads not only to
harmony between good persons but to harmony within the
soul of the good person himself. In so far as he is good he is
also likely to live, as the saying is, 'at peace with himself'.
On the other hand, the common view is that evil persons
cannot live peacefully together, or that in so far as they do
so it is because of the good in them. There is supposed to
be honour even amongst thieves.

If we couple with this popular connexion of goodness
with harmony, and of evil with conflict, the view that the
self-contradictory cannot exist, we may get some insight into
how it is that certain philosophers suppose themselves to

apprehend a necessary connexion between goodness and existence. The word 'contradictory' is often used as if it were synonymous with the word 'conflicting'. It may be said, for instance, of the policy of France, that it is self-contradictory, when it is meant that she is making an attempt to pursue two or more conflicting ends at the same time. There is, then, a natural tendency to confuse the conflicting with the self-contradictory, and if this confusion is once made it is always possible to talk of evil as self-contradictory. But it is also possible to deny existence to the self-contradictory, and therefore to deny existence to evil. Men, however, commonly suppose that evil exists; they believe that they often act from evil motives. If evil does not exist, they cannot really do so, but must merely imagine that they do so. Thus evil must be no more than an *appearance*.

The conclusion of our attempt to show that there is no necessary connexion between reality and goodness brings us naturally to a consideration of the distinction which Bosanquet makes between positive and negative freedom, for he tells us not only that the good will alone is real but also that it alone is free. He must therefore mean by freedom something more than absence of restraint by others. He of course makes it clear that he also means by it absence of this restraint, but he takes this to be a purely negative and inadequate meaning. In order to be positively free, the will must not only be free from restraint by others but also from restraint by one's own lower impulses, for this latter restraint, just as much as the former, prevents a man from being what he ought to be, a creature impelled to action by his higher impulses. Positive freedom, Bosanquet tell us, consists in the determination of the will by reason; it consists in the ability to act rationally, and the condition of its existence is as much absence of restraint by a man's own irrational impulses as absence of restraint by the actions of his neighbours.

The first thing that strikes us about Bosanquet's distinction is that it is grounded in the nature of the motives from which a man acts. If he acts from certain motives he is free, if he acts from others he is suffering constraint. Bosanquet, in fact, is using exactly the same criterion for distinguishing between free and unfree actions as we ordinarily use for distinguishing between good and evil ones. But, at the same time, he does not actually confuse goodness and freedom, any more than he confuses goodness and reality. The good will is free, not because it is good, but because good motives are the only ones which really belong to the self. According to Bosanquet restraint by irrational impulses is just as much external as is restraint by the actions of others.

Now the ordinary man would not allow that in the former case it is the self which is being restrained, for he would maintain that a man's lower impulses flow from his character just as much as his higher ones. What is restrained, he would say, is not his will, but merely his higher impulses, which, had not the lower existed, would have led to appropriate action.

It is difficult to see, in view of the fact that he asserts that the lower impulses do not really belong to the self, how Bosanquet can justify his distinction between positive and negative freedom. What appears to be freedom from restraint by the lower self is not freedom from restraint by anything which really belongs to the self. The so-called more adequate meaning of freedom now appears in its true light. It is the same as that which was formerly thought to be negative. Since the lower impulses do not properly belong to the self, to restrain them is not to control the self, but merely to ensure that the self is not restrained by something outside itself. Freedom is thus, once again, simply freedom from external restraint.

The truth is that Bosanquet cannot stick to both his assertions—that only the good self is real, and that 'positive' freedom consists in absence of restraint not merely by what is external to the self but also by what belongs to it and is, at the same time, evil. The Idealist account of freedom requires, if it is to be plausible, the reality of the lower impulses which it denies. To say that freedom consists in the motivation of the will by certain desires and not by others is not absurd. But to say that it is more than freedom from external constraint, since it also requires the absence of constraint by impulses which are only apparently real and are really external to the self, or rather non-existent, is to talk nonsense.

There is, of course, a distinction between positive and negative freedom to which Idealists often refer, but which has nothing at all to do with the peculiar theory that we have been discussing. Wherever there is freedom from constraint there is also freedom to act as one pleases. The freedom referred to is exactly the same in both cases but is regarded from two different angles. When we say that a man is free from constraint we assert that there is nothing to prevent his acting as he pleases. When we say that he is free to do what he likes we are asserting his ability to do so without having in mind its necessary condition, the absence of external restraint. But this quite ordinary distinction, although it is made so much of by the Idealists, obviously cannot help them to their ultimate conclusion that freedom consists in the determination of the will by rational desires. Before they can reach it they must, as they so often do, call in the assistance of metaphor and refer to irrational men as 'slaves to their lower impulses'. The fact that many men, more particularly those who have made it their business to improve the condition of their fellows, have had recourse to this metaphor proves only that one of the best ways of exciting in people a desire to alter their condition, whether moral or economical, is to persuade them that they are slaves to whatever it is of which their would-be benefactors wish them to be rid. However this may be, the proper distinction between positive and negative freedom does not make it possible to argue that absence of constraint by lower impulses, rather than by higher ones, constitutes freedom. Wickedness is just as much hampered by virtue as virtue by wickedness.

Much of what Bosanquet says gains plausibility from the fact that he nowhere gives an adequate account of what he means by the word 'will'. He talks of the real will, the general will, and the actual will, but he nowhere offers a description of their nature. He tells us only that the real will wills certain objects, that the general will wills these same objects, and that the actual will does not. He differentiates them in respect of the nature of their objects, but at the same time he implies that he is doing more than just classify different wishes. The will is not merely real in so far as it is determined to action by reason, and 'actual' in so far as it is not so determined. He speaks of the real will as if it were not identical with the actual will, but something quite separate from it. He suggests, therefore, that a difference in the nature of the objects of the will entails a difference in the will itself, so that it is not properly one will at all, but only appears to be so. The real will, he goes on to say, is 'the will which wills its own ends', or, in other words, 'the will which wills itself'. It can do so because *will* and *thought* are ultimately one and the same thing. As we have seen, in the opinion of Hegelians 'the will is a special way of thinking, it is thought translating itself into reality'.[1]

The assertion that the will is 'thought translating itself into reality' is, on the face of it, quite dogmatic.[2] It certainly is not got from experience, nor is it a necessary explanation of experience in the sense of an hypothesis constructed to make experience intelligible and subject to verification by it. On the other hand, it is certainly not self-evident. The

---

[1] Hegel, *Philosophy of Right*, p. 11.
[2] Its being meaningless could not, of course, as all historians know, deprive it of the right to be called dogmatic.

ordinary man recognizes a close connexion, in practice, between thinking and willing, but he also recognizes their absolute difference. When he is thinking he need not be willing as well, though he knows that thinking is a mental process which necessarily accompanies willing. Apart from thoughts and willings he knows nothing of thought and will.

In this case, as in many others, men have, for the sake of convenience, evolved words which suggest the existence of obscure entities. These latter, some of which are known as powers, forces, or faculties, are ordinarily supposed to be entities whose existence can be inferred from the occurrences whose causes they are supposed to be. For some reason or other it is supposed that these occurrences are unintelligible and impossible, except either as effects or *manifestations* of certain other entities which are either asserted to be everlasting or else to exist for a very much longer time than their effects. But, of course, what is given in experience can never be unintelligible or impossible, and there is never any need to postulate obscure entities in order to explain its existence.

It is the misfortune of philosophy that the convenience of ordinary men determines the evolution of language. As M. Nicod has pointed out, language, in order to cope with the extreme complexity of the world which it describes, must hide away much of it in the simplicity of the words which it invents to stand for very complicated facts. 'The mind', he says, 'remains attached to these new terms because of their aesthetic appeal. Thus the objective world becomes eclipsed by its representation; and . . . where we paint this picture, we must learn once more how to see the natural world.'[1] In this way language multiplies entities for its own convenience, so that philosophers, before they can even begin to describe the world, must perform that

[1] J. Nicod, *Foundations of Geometry* (International Library of Psychology, Kegan Paul), Introduction.

most difficult of all intellectual exercises, the skilful use of Occam's razor.

The Hegelians have been less modest than most men in their linguistic requirements. Where others have been content with one faculty they have insisted upon many. But, for all that, we must conclude, upon reflection, that there is no rational or real will of the kind that Bosanquet speaks of. If there is no such will, it follows that his account of *positive* freedom, which is based upon it, must also fall to the ground. We have dealt, therefore, with the third, fourth, and fifth propositions of our summary of Bosanquet's argument, and have now only the last two with which to deal. These latter run as follows: (6) The *real* will of one individual is numerically identical with the *real* wills of all individuals and is the same thing as the general will, which is an identity manifesting itself in difference and existing only as so manifested. (7) This *general will* is expressed in the law, so that it follows that the individual, when he appears to be forced to obey the law against his will, is really being forced to do what he wishes.

The nature of the identity-in-difference, which according to Bosanquet is the *general will*, he elucidates as follows:

'(i) Every social group is the external aspect of a set of corresponding mental systems in individual minds. (ii) Every individual mind is a system of such systems corresponding to the totality of social groups as seen from a particular position. (iii) The Social Whole, though implied in every mind, has reality only in the totality of minds in a given community considered as an identical working system.'[1]

This Social Whole Bosanquet treats not only as a system of minds, which it undoubtedly is, and a system whose members modify one another's characters profoundly in so far as they are members of it, but also as itself a mind possessing a will of its own. Moreover, the members of the system do not, as might be expected, stand to it in the

[1] Bosanquet, *Philosophical Theory of the State*, p. 170.

relation of parts to the whole which they compose, nor yet in the relation of particulars to the universal they particularize, but in some special relation of identity-in-difference, which enables them to be at the same time both the parts and the particulars of the general will which manifests itself in them and exists only in its manifestations. Indeed, the system is such that it may also be treated as an individual, so that its members are not only its parts and particulars, but also its phases. The social whole or identical working system, *implied*[1] in every mind and which constitutes the totality of such *implications*, may be identified with the *operative idea*, which, as the general will, is the ultimate reality of the state. But each social group is an operative idea as well, so that wherever a regular connexion of a specific character exists between a number of minds, we have *pro tanto* a general will. The state, therefore, is not the only social will; it is rather the most complete of them all, which includes the others within itself.

If then we discover the nature of a social group, we discover at the same time the nature of the state and of the general will. A social group is, says Bosanquet, the same thing as an organization. Now an organization is a system of minds which co-operate according to rules. This co-operation exists in order to promote certain ends which cannot be promoted at all, or, at least, not nearly so well, without it. It does not matter whether all those who co-operate have taken part in deciding upon the ends nor yet upon the means, so long as ends do exist and so long as the co-operation exists in order to promote them.

That which makes of the organization a system of minds is the existence of the ends which they co-operate to realize.

---

[1] Bosanquet's use of the words 'implied' and 'manifested' to refer to the relation which he supposes to subsist between a social whole and its members reminds one of the *reflections* which relate the universe and its constituent monads in Leibniz's *Monadology*. It might be said of the Leibnizian universe that it exists only in its manifestations (the monads), and of the monads that they are nothing apart from the universe, since they are merely manifestations (reflections) of it.

If the ends, or end, did not exist, there would, properly speaking, be no organization, though there might very well be association. The end is the external existence of a state of affairs which exists only in idea. That which is realized is the ideal state of affairs, and, in so far as action is needed before a reality corresponding to it can exist, it is perhaps legitimate to talk of it as an operative idea.

But this operative idea is not something which manifests itself in the activities of the persons who co-operate to realize it. The co-operation has, as one of its causes, the existence of the idea of the state of affairs which it is desired to realize in the minds of the persons who desire to realize it. So much is undeniable. But it does not follow from this that the existence of the idea is identical with the co-operation, in the sense that it is *manifested* in the latter and exists only as so *manifested*. Indeed, it is the very nature of such an idea that it exists already before the co-operation which is to realize it comes into being. What the co-operation is to do is to bring into existence something corresponding to the idea itself; nor can it, itself, constitute the reality of the idea. To a certain extent the phrase 'realizing the idea' is misleading. The real is that which exists. 'Realizing the idea' might therefore be taken to mean making the idea exist. This, however, is not properly what it means; that which is to be made real is not the idea, but something non-existent which, when brought into existence, will correspond to the idea. Yet if we are not quite clear in our minds as to what is meant by the phrase 'realizing an idea' we are very apt to delude ourselves into the belief that when we are willing we are 'translating subjectivity into objectivity' and that will is 'thought making itself real'. From this it is not a far step to the belief that when people are inspired to action by a common end they have also a common will, and that they could not have a common end unless they had also a common will.

Moreover, all the persons who co-operate within any

social group or organization do not necessarily consent to their co-operation, and therefore, *a fortiori*, do not recognize the end, for the promotion of which they co-operate, as common to them with others. Their motive for co-operation might be nothing other than fear of the consequences of not doing so. Though they would, as co-operators, necessarily be members of the social group, they would not possess real wills and consequently would have no part in the common will. The operative idea or general will would, therefore, not be manifested in them, and yet their co-operation would be a necessary condition of its realization. The existence of actual wills motivated by fear would then be necessary for the realization of that which alone ultimately exists, in contradistinction from these same actual wills which do not really exist at all.

Bosanquet, in his chapter on the 'Psychological Illustration of the Idea of a Real or General Will', makes a great deal of the fact that the individual mind is what it is chiefly because it has formed part of organizations or social groups which have profoundly modified it. This is certainly true, and it is also a very important truth, but it does not follow from it that the reality of the mind depends upon its being in constant association with other minds. That which explains the character of the mind does not necessarily explain its existence. Moreover, a system of minds is not itself what modifies the minds which compose it. It is the fact that minds are associated together and do modify one another which makes of these minds a system. The system is neither the cause nor the effect of the organization and mutual modification of minds; it is no more than the fact of their existence together and the effects of this togetherness upon them.

A criticism of Bosanquet's *real will* makes necessary some consideration of the *Identity-in-difference* or *Concrete Universality* which is supposed to constitute its nature. The *Concrete Universal* exists, we are told, only in its manifestations, but it is not merely their sum. In this it resembles the *Abstract Universal*, which exists only in its particulars and yet is not the aggregate of them but rather a qualitative identity which runs through them and in virtue of which they can be classed together. The Concrete Universal is, however, more than this. It is not merely a quality existing in the particular things which can be said to possess it, but also a single spiritual fact or idea *manifesting* itself in difference. It seems, therefore, that it is both a numerical and a qualitative identity. The differences or different things in which it manifests itself are at once its parts and its particulars.

Hobhouse accuses Bosanquet of confusing the universal with the individual. This accusation is not deserved. Bosanquet understands as well as any one the nature of what he calls 'abstract' universality. What he says of it is not that it is individuality, but that it is incomprehensible unless it is thought of as an abstraction from something more complete 'in which it finds its reality'. This more complete something is the *concrete universal*, which is, at the same time, universal and individual. Indeed, the Hegelians treat all the usually accepted categories as abstractions from the one fundamental one which is identity-in-difference. Universality, individuality, wholeness, causality, substance, and so on are all abstractions from identity. And just as identity is nothing apart from difference, so also the universal is nothing apart from its particulars, the individual apart from its phases, the whole apart from its parts, causation without particular causes and effects, and substance without qualities.

The criticism to be brought against Bosanquet is not that he confuses the categories, but that he does not understand that the differences between them are such that nothing is to be gained by making them mere aspects of something more fundamental than themselves. We may not understand them thoroughly, but we shall understand them no better by denying their essential difference from each other, and by making them no more than *manifestations* of some further category which is so far from making them intelligible that it is itself the least intelligible of them all. It also appears to be self-contradictory, in that it is impossible to conceive of a numerical identity which manifests itself in difference and which exists only in so far as it does so. Difference implies multiplicity, whereas identity implies unity. A whole must, of course, be composed of a multiplicity of parts, but it does not *manifest* itself in them. A unity whose nature it is to manifest itself as multiplicity, and which exists only because it is so manifested, is unthinkable. It is impossible for one thing to appear to be many things and yet to exist only in its appearance. Only an *abstract* universal can exist in the multiplicity of its particulars. It is its nature to be particularized and to have no existence outside its particulars, but it is certainly not 'manifested as a multiplicity'; that is to say, it appears in, but does not appear to be, many things.

Moreover, the difference between the categories is none the less absolute for the fact that the same thing may be, at the same time, an instance of several of them. A single thing may be at once a particular, a whole, a part, and an individual, but it does not follow from this that its character as a particular is the same as its character as a whole, or as a part, or as any of its other determinations.

It is significant that, though Bosanquet does not actually confuse identity-in-difference with the other categories, but supposes it to be something more fundamental in which their contradictions are *reconciled*, he yet never explains its nature except in terms of them. He uses, of course, certain vague phrases which help to blind us, and himself as well, to this fact. His language at one moment prompts us to believe that he is talking about the relation between a whole and its parts, at another that he is referring to that between a universal and its particulars, and so on throughout the whole list of the categories. And yet, since we are never sure exactly what it is that he is talking about, but none the less believe that he must be talking about something, we are apt, in our unguarded moments, to take it for granted that there really is some such fundamental category which is not the same as any of the others but is somehow a combination of them all.

We have said enough perhaps to convince the reader who is not an Idealist that there can be no such thing as identity-in-difference, and consequently no such thing as the general will, if it is supposed to be an instance of it. The sixth proposition of our summary of Bosanquet's main argument, the one which identifies the individual's *rational* or *real* will with the *general* will of the community, has therefore been proved to be false, and it only remains to us, for the sake of completeness, to deal with the seventh.

This last proposition asserts that the general will is expressed in the law, so that what the law enjoins is precisely what the individual really wishes to do. The law, being the embodiment of the general will, must also embody the individual's real will, since it is the same thing as the general will, so that the law never really interferes with the freedom of the persons who appear to be coerced in its name.

Now, since it is clear that there is no such thing as a *real* or *general* will, it follows that the law cannot be an expression of it. We have not, therefore, to criticize the seventh proposition of our summary as it stands, since this would be a superfluous task, but need only consider whether the law is the embodiment of reason, that is to say, whether what it commands us to do is precisely what we should wish to do were our motives for action always rational. Stated in this way, the problem immediately loses its philosophical character and becomes purely empirical.

We need not be cynics to suggest that the laws and customs of even the most enlightened countries are far from being the embodiment of reason, for they do not, if obeyed, tend to bring into existence what completely reasonable men would desire under the circumstances. Bosanquet, indeed, sees the difficulty of reconciling his theory of the nature of law with the undoubted fact that all governments enforce bad laws. He therefore goes on to tell us that all laws do not express the general will, but that good ones alone do so. But, since we believe that we have shown that the general will cannot exist, we can attach no more meaning to Bosanquet's opinions with regard to the law than that he believes that all good laws are rational in the sense that if obeyed they would tend to bring into existence what reasonable men would desire under the circumstances. This truism will not be disputed.

If, however, Bosanquet assumes that most laws are rational, and that therefore the law as a whole provides men with a systematic interference with their freedom which nearly always tends to make them better than they were, then it is no longer possible to agree with him. Laws, customs, and social conventions are not the least of the causes which have developed and made permanent in men some of the most unpleasant qualities which civilization has brought to light. The laws of property and the social conventions, for instance, make permanent class-distinctions, which often give rise to arrogance and indifference in the wealthy and to hatred and envy in the poor. So also the past inferior status of women, as well as some of their peculiar defects, were the consequences of bad laws which have not long been repealed in even the most advanced countries. These laws were justified by philosophers, legislators, and religious teachers, who looked upon women as hardly superior to children.[1]

Laws have, of course, played their indispensable part in civilizing men, but no one doubts that civilized man might

[1] It is curious that dramatists, novelists, and other persons whose main interest has been human nature have hardly ever believed in the inferiority of women.

have been a very much better person than he is had the laws which civilized him themselves been better. Nor is it a criticism of this contention to assert that the laws of any age are probably the best which the men of that time can be expected to make. Such, indeed, may sometimes have been the case, which fact does not make the laws and customs in question any more likely to bring into existence what perfectly reasonable men would desire under the circumstances. Indeed, so far are we from believing that laws and customs are the embodiments of reason that we are always agitating to have them altered, being inspired to do so by the wise men of our time, whom we suppose to be wiser than the law. Under an autocratic or oligarchic government the laws are likely to be little better than the worst which the governed will endure; under a democratic government they are likely to reflect the wishes of the majority of the citizens, who, being many of them of limited intelligence as well as ignorant and misinformed, are quite often poor judges of their own interests and of the most efficient means to promote them.

The general political theory of Bosanquet, which is also, in the main, that of Hegel, has now been considered as completely as was thought necessary. The conclusion arrived at has been that there cannot exist a real or general will such as they describe, so that they have not proved that when an individual does what the government orders him to do against his apparent wish he is really doing what he wishes. The Idealist theory of implicit consent, as an explanation of why it is the duty of the subject to obey the government, falls to the ground, and with it the most complicated and obscure of all attempts to base political obligation upon consent alone. The nature of the relation between consent and political obligation, which it is the object of this book to discover, has still to be found.

CHAPTER III
THE COMMON GOOD

IN addition to the theory discussed in the last chapter there has been evolved a further theory of political obligation which has been fairly widely accepted and which has also been constructed with a view to avoiding the difficulties which lay in the path of the contract theorists. This theory, unlike the Hegelian one, rejected consent as a primary basis of political obligation and substituted for it the notion of a common good. It maintained that the only fact which justified obedience to the government on the part of the governed was the promotion by the former of some good which was common to all the persons who owed obedience to it.

We must consider this theory, at least in broad outline, because, if we were to accept it as true, we should have to qualify the conclusions at which we ultimately arrive. If the common good should turn out to be the only basis of political obligation, then it follows that there is no relation between the obedience which a subject owes to his government and the fact of his consent to its actions, excepting only an indirect one to the extent to which such consent is a means to the common good. The existence of this indirect relation is, indeed, an integral part of the theory which we are discussing, but no consideration of it is necessary until the main doctrine has been dealt with and unless it has been found to be true.

This doctrine is best expounded in T. H. Green's *Lectures on Political Obligation*, although, in order to gain a better understanding of it, it will also be necessary to have recourse to his *Prolegomena to Ethics*. Indeed, the theory is so much Green's that a study of these two books alone is sufficient to enable the student to attain to an adequate understanding of it.

'The State', he tells us, 'is an institution for the promotion of a common good.'[1]

'Because a group of beings are capable each of conceiving an absolute good of himself and of conceiving it to be good for himself as identical with, and because identical with, the good of the rest of the group, there arises for each a consciousness that the common good should be the object of action.'[2]

'What is certain is that a habit of subjection founded upon . . . fear, could not be a basis of political or free society; for to this it is necessary . . . that it should represent an idea of common good, which each member of the society can make his own so far as he is rational, i.e. capable of the conception of a common good.'[3]

It is clear, from these quotations, that the duty to obey the government depends entirely, for Green, upon the success with which it promotes a certain end. Indeed, he would hold that the duty to overthrow the government and the duty to obey it both derive from the same source, the general duty to promote the common good. It may be true, of course, that the overthrow of governments would, in the majority of cases, do less to promote the common good than to diminish it, but it would be true, nevertheless, that if the opposite were the case it would be the duty of the governed to rid themselves of their rulers. Thus, in so far as his theory enables him to account for the obligation to revolt as readily as he accounts for the obligation to obey, it possesses obvious advantages over the theories of Hegel and Bosanquet.

It is, however, when we come to try to discover the nature of the common good which is supposed to be the end of the State that we find ourselves in difficulties. What is this good which the State exists to promote? How can it be common to several people? What is meant by the word 'common' in this context? Indeed, what does Green mean by 'my' and 'your' in such phrases as 'my' good and 'your' good? To what kind of possession do these possessive adjectives refer? Is 'my' feeling of pleasure mine exactly in the same sense

[1] *Lectures on Political Obligation*, p. 131.
[2] Ibid., p. 47. [3] Ibid., p. 126.

as 'my' shoes are? And, even if Green can answer these questions satisfactorily, even if, in fact, there does exist a common good which it is the duty of the State to promote, why should this be the sole duty of the State? Are there not other good things as well, besides such as are common to several persons? If there are, why should it not be the duty of the State to promote them also? Either, for Green, there are no goods of this nature or else, if there are, they are such that it is impossible for the State to promote their existence, so that it cannot be its duty to do so.

The good which it is the duty of the State to promote is, according to Green, the moral qualities of its members. This is made quite clear by his insistence that

'The value, then, of [the] institutions of civil life lies in their operation as giving reality to [the] capacities of will and reason, and enabling them to be exercised. In their general effect, apart from particular aberrations, they render it possible for a man to be freely determined by the idea of a possible satisfaction of himself, instead of being driven this way and that by external forces, and thus they give reality to the capacity called will: and they enable him to realize his reason, i.e. his idea of self-perfection, by acting as a member of a social organisation in which each contributes to the better-being of the rest.'[1]

The State, however, cannot promote this end directly. It does so only through the maintenance of the institutions of civil life. As the sustainer of rights and the enforcer of obligations, it maintains in existence a state of affairs which makes possible the moral development of its members. But, whether it can promote this end directly or indirectly, it still remains true that it exists only in order to promote it. Green does not allow that an institution which does not exist in order to maintain this good is properly a state. 'We only count Russia a state by a sort of courtesy on the supposition that the power of the Czar, though subject to no constitutional control, is so far exercised in accor-

[1] *Lectures on Political Obligation*, p. 32.

dance with a recognized tradition of what the public good requires, as to be, on the whole, a sustainer of rights.'[1]

Green is not satisfied with telling us that the common good which the State exists to promote consists in the moral development of its members. He also attempts to tell us what this moral development itself consists in. 'The true development of man . . . consists in so living that the objects in which self-satisfaction is habitually sought, contribute to the realisation of a true idea of what is best for man.'[2] 'As his [man's] true good is or would be their [his will's and his reason's] complete realization, so his goodness is proportionate to his habitual responsiveness to the idea of there being such a true good. . . . In other words, it consists in the direction of the will to objects determined for it by this idea.'[3] It is not necessary here carefully to consider, still less to attempt to attach any meaning to, such phrases as 'the complete realization' of a man's will and his reason. In so far as they exist, they are real, and therefore have no need of realization.

But what does interest us in this definition of moral development is the fact that it really involves a circle. If we ask, What is man's true good? we are told that it consists in the realization of his will and his reason. But, at the same time, his goodness is said to consist in his 'responsiveness to the idea of there being such a true good'. What, then, does this phrase 'responsiveness to the idea' mean? Is it fair to suppose that a man is 'responsive to the idea' in this sense when his will is determined to action by the apprehension of the idea? If we take the passages quoted above literally, the phrase 'in other words' clearly suggests that 'responsiveness to the idea' is then meant to be the same thing as 'the direction of the will to objects determined for it by this idea'. But it is also clear that the goodness of the man *consists in* this direction of the will.

[1] Ibid., p. 137.
[2] *Prolegomena to Ethics*, section 177.   [3] Ibid., section 180.

Green therefore, in this instance, equates the goodness of the individual with *the complete realization* of certain of his capacities, and also with a *responsiveness to the idea* that such a realization would be good. It follows from this that a man's capacities are completely *realized* when he is *responsive to the idea* that such a realization would be good. Hence, since a man's goodness is the same thing as his responsiveness to a certain idea, which latter is the same thing as a realization of certain of his capacities, it is evident that the good man is the man who is responsive to the idea that responsiveness to the idea that responsiveness to the idea . . . (and so on *ad infinitum*) is his greatest good.

The only possible objection to this criticism is that it equates a man's *true good* with his *goodness*. It is not his *true* good, it may be said, but his goodness, which consists in his responsiveness to the idea of his true good. It is, of course, undeniable that it is a legitimate inference from Green's use of the phrase 'true good' that he intended to mean by it something different from what he intended to mean by the word 'good'. For if he thought it necessary to speak of a true good he may have done so because he wanted to distinguish it from a good which he thought was not a 'true' good.

Whatever Green's reasons for the use of this phrase, it is clear that nothing is added to the idea of goodness by the qualification he has in mind. All good things are true goods, in the sense that any one who asserted of them that they are good would be making a true statement. Actually the property of being true does not belong to the good things themselves, but only to statements made about them which assert that they possess certain properties which, in fact, they do possess. To say that anything which is not a statement is true is merely an elliptical way of saying that certain statements about it, when made, would be true. If, then, Green thinks that some goods are not true goods, he must mean that they are not really goods at all, in the sense that all statements made about them asserting that they possess the property of being good would be false. If he does not mean this, he means nothing, for this is the only possible meaning of his words.

If, in the present case, a distinction is to be made between a man's true good and his goodness, it is evident that it can be made only on the ground that his goodness is not really goodness at all, but merely appears to be so. This, however, would involve us in a deliberate misinterpretation of Green's moral theory. If there is one thing that he continually asserts to be good without qualification, it is this 'responsiveness' to the idea of a true good. Indeed, he equates this 'responsiveness' with virtue and then goes on to tell us that virtue is the highest good, in fact, the common good which it is the only duty of the State to promote.[1] And it is in this virtue that the *true* good of the individual consists, for he also tells us that the end of the State is the promotion of the *self-perfection* or *true* good of its members.

If we consider how, according to Green, the members of society acquire their moral qualities, we see how it is that he comes to involve himself in this difficulty. He tells us 'that only through a recognition by certain men of a common interest, and through the expression of that recognition in certain regulations of their dealings with each other, could morality originate, or any meaning be gained for such terms as "ought" and "right" and their equivalents'.[2] Now, from a consideration of many passages in both the *Lectures* and the *Prolegomena*, it is clear that he regards the phrase *common interest* as synonymous with *common good*. Moreover, he defines moral personality as 'the capacity on the part of an individual for making a common good his own'.[3] A moral person, then, must be a person capable of having rights and able to understand the meaning of the word

---

[1] *Prolegomena to Ethics*, Book III, chap. IV, sects. 240–5: 'Virtue as the Common Good'.
[2] *Lectures on Political Obligation*, p. 124.   [3] Ibid., p. 45.

'ought'. Moral personality—the ability to be a subject of rights and to act from a sense of moral obligation—arises only 'through a recognition by certain men of a common interest', and consists in the capacities that they acquire 'for making a common good their own'.

It would seem, then, on the evidence of the above passages, that the existence of the common good is prior to the existence of moral persons. This conclusion, however, is contradicted by every assertion which Green makes to the effect that the end of the State—the common good which it exists to promote—consists in the moral perfection of its members. Now Green is just as insistent that moral personality consists in the capacity for being determined to action by a desire to promote the common good as he is that the common good consists in the development of moral personality. It is not merely that he can, on rare occasions, be found to be making both these assertions. On the contrary, he is constantly repeating them, often both on the same page, as if they were quite indispensable to his theory and as if the truth of one of them necessarily followed from the truth of the other.

The next matter into which we must inquire, if we are to deal clearly and adequately with Green's theory, concerns the various meanings of the words 'common', 'my', 'your', and so on, in such phrases as 'common good', 'my 'good', and 'your good'. How exactly do these adjectives qualify the nouns to which they are attached? What is the nature of the property to which a man refers by the word 'my' when he makes such a statement as 'this is my good'?

In the first place, it is clear that a 'common' good must be such that several people can truly assert that it is theirs. For instance, if a good is common to A and to B, then the two statements made about it—'This is A's good' and 'This is B's good'—must be true, even if they are made at exactly the same time. That is to say, if the good, in being A's, could not at the same time be B's, it could not be common to them. Indeed, when we say that a good is common to *A* and *B*, we mean no more than that it is both *A*'s good and *B*'s. We should not mean, and Green does not mean, that there are two goods in question, exactly similar, one of which is *A*'s and the other *B*'s. We are considering one good and one good only, so that the good which is *A*'s is numerically identical with the good which is *B*'s. That this is a fair interpretation of Green's meaning is made evident by the passage which runs: 'Because a group of beings are capable each of conceiving an absolute good of himself and of conceiving it to be good for himself as identical with, and because identical with, the good of the rest of the group, there arises for each a consciousness that the common good should be the object of action.'[1] If, then, we wish to know what Green means by the word 'common' in this context, we must first find out what he means by the words 'my', 'your', and so on, in similar contexts.

Words such as 'my', 'your', and 'his' are possessive adjectives. When a man says that anything is *his* he is asserting that there exists some special relation between him and the thing which he calls *his*. This relation is the relation of possession, in virtue of which a man can be said to possess what is acknowledged to be *his*.

This relation of possession, the existence of which is asserted whenever any statements embodying possessive adjectives are made, is not, however, really one relation at all. That is to say, the relation which a man asserts to exist between himself and one object when he calls it *his* is not necessarily the same as that which he asserts to exist between himself and another object when he calls it *his*. For instance, the relation between *A* and *his* shoes, referred to in the sentence 'These are *A*'s shoes', is quite different in kind from that between him and his enjoyment of something pleasant referred to in the sentence 'This is *A*'s pleasure'. Yet *A*, if he wished to inform any one that there existed

[1] *Lectures on Political Obligation*, p. 47.

either of these two very different relations between himself and some object, would use the same word 'my' to convey his meaning in both cases. He would do so because he could not do otherwise. Language, which so often provides us with synonyms where none are needed, as often compels us to use the same word in several different meanings.

Indeed, the two relations mentioned above are not the only ones that are habitually referred to by the use of possessive adjectives, although they comprise, perhaps, their two most important meanings. Mr. Augustus John can still intelligibly refer to certain pictures that he has painted as *his*, although, in fact, they are now the legal property of other persons. Again, few Germans are offended when Hitler informs them that the Germans are *his* people, though they might very well take offence if they imagined that he intended them to understand that they were *his* in the sense in which his shoes are *his*, or in which his anger is *his*, or even in the sense in which *Mein Kampf* is *his*. It is possible to give yet other instances of the use of possessive adjectives where their meanings are again different from what they are in any of the above examples. It is not, however, necessary to go into all this detail, except only to remark that it exists, and that it is, therefore, important to bear its existence in mind when we come to consider what exactly it is that Green means when he says that a *good* is common to several people, in the sense that each of them can truly say that it is *his* good.

It is clear, from the first, that the relation between a man and *his* good to which Green is referring is not legal possession. He does not suppose that a man's self-perfection is *his* in the same sense in which his shoes are *his*. Legal possession, the legal right to the use of certain objects, can exist only where some man, or some body of men, in consequence of the fact that their commands are habitually obeyed by the persons whom they intend should obey them, have the power to protect their subjects in their use of these objects. No man, however, can use his self-perfection in this sense, so that he cannot be protected in its use. Nor yet does his self-perfection cease to be *his* if he lives amongst men who are not in the habit of obeying any particular man or body of men. It may be true, of course, that his self-perfection (i.e. his being what he ought to be) is a property which he would never have acquired unless he had lived amongst men who are in the habit of an obedience of this sort. None the less, having once acquired the property in this way, he might still retain it even if he ceased to live amongst men of this kind. On the other hand, life amongst such men is obviously the condition not only of acquiring but also of retaining the legal right to the use of certain objects. Moreover, even if life amongst such people is the condition of acquiring both legal property and also the property of being moral, yet the methods of acquisition in the two cases are entirely distinct. A mere command of the government can give us the legal right to the use of anything, so long as it has the power to protect us in this use. No such command, however, can give us moral perfection. The meanings of the word 'property' in these two cases are entirely distinct.

In what sense, then, is a man's moral perfection *his*? It is obviously *his* in the same sense as a perception of pleasure, an act of will, or an apprehension is *his*. It is *his* in the sense that it is a state or modification of his mind.[1] Moral perfection, or virtue, is nothing other than a tendency on the part of a man's will to be determined to action by the desire to act rightly. It is, therefore, a property of the mind, not in the sense that it is something which the mind has the right to use, something which belongs to it, but in the sense that it is something which is a quality of it. Similarly, whenever we talk of a man's knowledge or pleasure we are alluding to

---

[1] This is not intended to imply any special theory as to the nature of mind. The phrase 'a state of mind' is used in the ordinary plain meaning which philosophers must analyse, but cannot deny.

an apprehension of a fact, and a perception of a pleasant feeling, which are activities of the mind which he is. We are not concerned, here, with the question whether the pleasant feeling is itself a state of his mind. If it is not, then he can call it *his* only because it is the object of an apprehension which is a state of his mind.

Most, if not all, of the things which we call good are, as a matter of fact, states of somebody or other's mind. Virtue, knowledge, affection, consciousness of pleasant feelings and of beautiful objects are amongst the things that are almost universally recognized to be good. They are all of them states of the mind, and, as such, they can never be states of more than one mind. Indeed, it is incompatible with the very nature of most of the things which we know are good to be common to two or more persons. For the very reason that they are states of mind, they can be states of one mind only.

It follows, then, that the particular good (virtue) which Green supposed to be the end of the State, and, therefore, the common good for the promotion of which it exists, is precisely such that it cannot be common. The fact of its being one man's good excludes the possibility of its also being other men's good.

Of course, the fact that the good of which Green speaks must necessarily be a private good does not mean that it must be good only *for* the person whose private good it is. In other words, its being a private good does not mean that it is the duty of nobody but the person whose good it is to promote it. It is not private in the sense implied by egoistic hedonists when they argue from the fact that a man's pleasure is his own to its being nobody's duty but his to promote it. In so far as it is at all a duty to promote the existence of what is good, it is every one's duty to promote it, whoever's good it may be. In this sense all good is common and public, but this, unfortunately, is not the sense in which Green supposed that it was.

It would be no defence of Green to assert that, when he says a good is common to a number of people, he really means no more than that it is the duty of those people to promote it, whether or not it happens to be a state or an activity of their own minds. Such a defence would involve an entire misinterpretation of his theory. A good is not, according to him, common to several people because it is the duty of all of them to promote it; it is their duty to promote it because it is a good common to them.

Green often speaks of a man's interest in another's good, which he has made his own, as if it were a disinterested interest. This fact would, in itself, lend support to the view that Green means us to understand that the good is common to the two men in question only in the sense that it is the duty of both of them to promote it. This is obviously the only meaning of the word 'common' which could possibly allow of the first man's interest being disinterested. The end of the State could then be taken to be nothing other than the greatest good of the greatest number, though, of course, this good would not consist only of happiness. No doubt this would be a sounder view than the one which we have alleged to be advocated by Green. But unfortunately we cannot suppose, against the great mass of evidence which supports it, that our allegation is false. On the contrary, we must assume that Green's views as to what constitutes the good and as to what its being common to several people consists in would, if true, preclude the possibility of any man's having a genuinely disinterested interest in another man's good.

The truth is that Green was not himself uninfluenced by the theories of the cruder hedonists. He contended, of course, that pleasure is not the only good, but he seems to have found it difficult to reconcile himself to the view that it can be a man's duty to promote what does not in any way benefit himself. This is what is, at bottom, behind his attempt to make out that what appears at first sight to be merely a private good is in reality common to a large number of people. This is why he often appears anxious to reconcile the principles of self-love and benevolence. In actual fact, he is so anxious to reconcile them that he almost goes so far as to deny any fundamental distinction between them. In his hands benevolence seems to become nothing other than particularly enlightened and foresighted self-love.

All this is made clear in a variety of passages in the *Prolegomena to Ethics*, of which the following is typical:

'it is a man's thought of himself as permanent which gives rise to the idea of such a good (i.e. a social good not private to the man himself), and . . . the thought of himself as permanent is inseparable from an identification of himself with others, in whose life he contemplates himself as living. . . . Hence the distinction commonly supposed to exist between considerate benevolence and reasonable Self-Love, as co-ordinate principles on which moral approbation is founded, is a fiction of philosophers . . . the distinction between good for self and good for others has never entered into that idea of a true good in which moral judgements are founded.'[1]

The conclusion, then, is that moral qualities could not exist, except amongst persons interested in a common good.

No one, according to Green, could be interested in another's good unless he thought of the other as identical with himself. When he has done this, he is in a position to think of the other's good as his own, and so to be interested in its promotion. Green further thinks that it is only when he lives in a society in which each person regards his own recognition of certain claims made by his fellows as the condition of their recognition of similar claims on his part, that a man can acquire the capacity to identify himself with his fellows and so to interest himself in their good in such a way as to make it his own.

It is, however, at once apparent that one man's thinking another man's good to be his own will not actually make it so. If another's good is really to be common to the other

---

[1] *Prolegomena to Ethics*, p. 279, section 232.

with himself, he must not only think of himself as identical with the other, but he must, in fact, be identical with him. This is necessary because there is no other way in which a state of the other can, at the same time, be a state of himself.

A fair interpretation of his theory should make it clear that Green is never actually prepared to assert that a man, in identifying himself with another, in fact becomes identical with him. On the contrary, he always insists that the difference between the persons interested in the common good is real and must always be accepted as such. He is so careful to insist upon this that he makes it impossible for himself to give any satisfactory explanation of how such a good as the one which he thinks it is the duty of the State to promote can be common to several people.

It should not be difficult, at this stage, to see why it is that Green considers the common good to be the only one which it is the duty of the state to promote. Though he does not admit it, it is clear that he finds it difficult to understand how a man can possibly wish to promote a good which is not his own. On the other hand, he is aware of the fact that men often do wish to promote other men's good, and so, in order to avoid the difficulty, he concludes that it must at the same time be their good also. In this way he finds himself obliged to maintain that the only good, for the promotion of which men might conceivably co-operate within the State, must be common to them all. Otherwise he does not understand why they should co-operate, except from merely prudential motives in so far as they might find that only by co-operating with others could they achieve their own private goods. But, if their motives for co-operating with others in this way consisted merely in the desire to promote their private goods, they would be treating their fellow men as means only and not also as ends. Green, if he held this view, would be in very much the same position as Hobbes, excepting only that he would not consider pleasure to be the sole good. He saw, however, that if he held this view, he would also have to hold that the existence of much that is considered of the greatest moral worth in human activity is illusory; and this he was unwilling to do. He had, then, no alternative but to put forward a theory which would make it possible for a man to be interested in the promotion of other men's good without ever being interested in a good which was not his own. The notion of a common good was needed to explain away the difference between the principles of reasonable self-love and benevolence, which Green, for all his criticism of the egoists, supposed to be mutually antagonistic and irreconcilable on any other terms.

Before we end our consideration of Green's theory it would be just as well to look into his account of the nature of the moral personality, which is the common good which alone can be promoted by the State. This moral personality he defines not only as responsiveness to the idea that there is a common good, which, as we have seen, ends nowhere and is not properly a definition at·all, but also as virtue, or, in other words, the tendency of the will to be determined to action by a certain kind of desire.

Now it is evident that virtue, defined in this way, cannot be the only good which exists, even if, in fact, it is the only one which it is the duty of the State to promote. For 'the common characteristic of the good is that it satisfies some desire',[1] whereas 'the moral good [is] that which satisfies the desire of a moral agent, or that in which a moral agent can find the satisfaction of himself which he necessarily seeks'.[2] Moreover, it is clear that, in view of the fact that it is every one's duty to promote the existence of what is good to the best of his ability, the only reason why the State should promote virtue and not any other good is that it is the only good which it is capable of promoting, because it is the only good which can possibly be common to a number of people.

---

[1] *Prolegomena to Ethics*, p. 201, section 171.
[2] Ibid., p. 202, section 171.

The desire which determines the virtuous will does not, according to Green, consist in the desire for any particular object, but rather in the desire to promote the greatest possible satisfaction of all other desires. The morally perfect man, the man of virtue, whose will and reason are as they ought to be, is he who regulates his life in such a way as to ensure the greatest possible satisfaction, and the least possible dissatisfaction, of desires both for himself and for others. It does not matter what the natures of the desires to be satisfied are, so long as they are satisfied and so long as the satisfaction of them does not tend to arouse in the mind further desires which cannot, in fact, be satisfied. The satisfaction of desire, that is, the bringing into existence of its object, is the same thing as goodness, so that no desire can be evil, except only in the sense that it is a desire which is not capable of satisfaction, or else one which, even when it is satisfied, tends to give birth to others which cannot be so. Indeed, strictly speaking, no desire can be either good or evil in itself, but only a means to that which is intrinsically good or evil the satisfaction or non-satisfaction of itself.

Virtue, or prudence, as some critics would prefer to call what Green calls virtue, being no more than a tendency of the mind to be determined to action by a certain kind of desire, can be neither good nor evil in itself. It can be no more than the most efficient of all means to the attainment of the greatest possible amount of what is good in itself. Whether it really is so or not is a matter which it is not necessary to go into here, but even if it happened that it were, it still would not deserve the title of supreme good, the only good thing which is good without qualification. This title may be deserved by Kant's good will, but not by Green's virtue, which, for all its author's opinions to the contrary, is not by any means the same thing.

It may be objected to this criticism of Green that it does not take into account the possibility that he may have meant virtue to be good not only as a means to the production of desires likely to be satisfied, but also as itself the satisfaction of some ulterior desire. This ulterior desire would be the desire to desire the greatest possible satisfaction of all desires. There is, however, no evidence that Green ever assumed the existence of any such desire, and therefore no evidence that he had any right to consider virtue, in his meaning of that word, as good in itself. Moreover, as a matter of psychology, it is doubtful whether the will is ever, except perhaps on very rare occasions, determined by any such desire. Even if in fact it is, Green makes no use of it to make more plausible his contention that virtue is the supreme good. It is obvious that when he talks of virtue in this way, he is talking of it not as itself a satisfaction of an ulterior desire, but as itself a desire. In doing so he is obviously rejecting his own definition of goodness, for he is saying that its goodness consists not in its being a satisfaction of a desire, nor yet in its tendency to promote the greatest possible satisfaction of desires, but in its being the particular kind of desire which it is (or rather, the tendency to be determined by that particular kind of desire).

The satisfaction of desire, which Green equates with goodness, is not, he is careful to insist, the same thing as the pleasure which usually attends the successful attainment of its object. This pleasure, so far from being the same thing as the satisfaction, is merely an effect of it. The satisfaction itself must consist either in the actual attainment of the object of desire, or else in something which happens to the desire as a result of this attainment. It is not quite clear which of the two it is, but it is probable that it is the latter rather than the former. This, at least, is the conclusion to which everyday language points, for when we say, 'If he gets what he wants, he will be satisfied', we do not suppose that we are saying nothing more informative than, 'If he gets what he wants, he will get what he wants'. The most obvious thing which happens to a desire upon the attainment of its object is its own annihilation, so that it is likely that the satisfaction of desire and its annihilation in a particular way are one and the same thing. All annihilation of desire is not, of course, equivalent to satisfaction; it is equivalent to it only when it is the direct result of the attainment of the object of desire.

It appears, then, that the common good of the members of the State is the same thing as the development in each of them of a tendency to be determined to action by the desire to promote the greatest possible number of annihilations of desires, provided only that they result from the attainment of their objects. This, at least, is what the common good should consist in, if Green is to remain true to his own premisses. On his own terms, there is no other meaning that can be attached to moral personality or virtue. It cannot be anything intrinsically good, but, at the best, nothing more than the most efficient of all means to what is intrinsically good, i.e. to the annihilation of desire resulting from the attainment of its object.

There is not much doubt that Green would have been as dissatisfied with this definition of the common good as any one else. It is, on the face of it, hardly deserving of being erected into the be-all and end-all of every legitimate governmental activity. Clearly, virtue cannot be adequately described as prudence, and the mere annihilation of desire, so far from being the only true good, is good only to the extent to which it makes possible the avoidance of the pain which usually attends unsatisfied desire. Indeed, there are few better reasons for presuming the falseness of certain opinions than the fact that they are avoided even by the persons who are logically committed to them. In spite of the fact that his own theory requires that virtue should be good only as a means, Green insists that it is the highest of all intrinsic goods. From false premisses he arrives at a correct conclusion, and so, at the price of inconsistency, still retains something of the truth.

Enough has been said about Green's theory in the attempt to show that it is false. If the arguments advanced against it are accepted, the conclusion that there can be no such thing as a common good is unavoidable. It is, of course, obvious that one man's good can be the object of many men's desires, and therefore the end of many men's actions. But it does not follow from this that the good which is a common end is also a common good. Co-operation, many men's acting together for the attainment of the same end, necessarily involves the existence of common ends. One man's action is always a different action from his neighbour's, so that no two men can ever take part in the same action. They can, however, co-operate, so long as their separate actions are means to the same end.

The meaning of the word 'common' in the phrase 'common end' is different from, though related to, its meaning in the phrase 'common good'. An end is not *common* to a number of persons in the sense of being at the same time a state of each of their minds, but only in the sense of being related to similar states of each of their minds. These states are, of course, the desires of which the end in question is the object. There is only one end, but there are many desires of which it is the object, and its being 'common' consists in its being related in a special way to all these desires at once.

The important but, perhaps, rather obvious truth upon which Green is insisting throughout his *Lectures on Political Obligation*, and also his *Prolegomena to Ethics*, is that the promotion of all good, particularly virtue, depends to a large extent upon co-operation and social intercourse. No one will deny that a man who from his earliest infancy lived entirely alone on some desert island would miss most of the most valuable things in life. He would possess few, if any, of the qualities of a moral and intellectual being, even if, in fact, nature had endowed him more liberally than any man who ever had the advantage of living in civilized society.

Green's mistake was not in insisting on this important psychological and sociological truth, but in using it to support a false and logically impossible political theory. He failed to distinguish a common end which is a private good from a common good, and he failed to do so because he did not properly analyse the meaning of his words.

CHAPTER IV

RIGHTS

NO adequate theory of the relation of consent to political obligation is possible unless it includes a consideration of the nature of rights. We must, therefore, find out, if we can, in what rights consist and, more especially, why a certain number of persons, known collectively as the Government, are generally acknowledged to have the right to make and to enforce laws which it is supposed to be the duty of certain other persons, their subjects, to obey. In this present chapter we will confine ourselves to the more general of these two major problems, and leave the other for consideration in a later chapter. We will attempt no more than to define rights, to differentiate between their more important kinds, and to criticize one or two theories concerning them which we believe to be false.

We will begin with a definition. A right is a power which a creature ought to possess, either because its exercise by him is itself good or else because it is a means to what is good, and in the exercise of which all rational beings ought to protect him. A man, for instance, cannot have a right to such physical strength as would enable him to move mountains without the aid of tools, but he can have a right to express his opinions freely even when his fellow men, or a certain powerful company of them, conspire to deprive him of the power to do so. This distinction is necessary to make it clear that rights are always held against rational creatures, since these alone are capable of the corresponding obligations. It does not suffice that a creature's exercise of a certain power should be good or else a means to the good to establish its right to it, since there may be no rational beings against whom it might possess it. A man, for instance, can only have the right to do what it is possible for him to do provided other men actively help him or else do not prevent him from doing it. Rights, since they imply obligations, can be held only against creatures capable of the conception of duty; but, on the other hand, they may be held by creatures not capable of it provided only that they come into contact with those which are.

Rights, in general, are of three kinds. They are either powers which ought to be secured to creatures because the exercise of them is itself good, or else such as ought to be secured to them because their exercise is a necessary means to the existence of what is good, or finally such as ought to be secured to them because they have been granted them by persons who have the right to grant them. It is obvious that all rights must fall into one of these categories, and there is no reason why any particular right should not fall into all three or into any two of them. Legal rights are merely such of the powers that men ought to have as their governors are prepared to secure to them even by the use of force.

The third kind of right that we have just defined is not really a different kind from the second, although it is convenient to treat it as if it were. A man whose title to a certain power depends upon some one else's having granted it to him possesses it either because its exercise by him is a means to the existence of some further good, or else because it is a means to the existence of the good which consists in the exercise of his ultimate right by the grantor. To take an instance which will illustrate this latter case, let us suppose that a man ought to be able to do what he wishes with the fruits of his own labour so long as he does not use them to harm other people. Let us suppose also that this is a power he ought to have because the exercise of it is good in itself. Then, there being no other considerations relevant to the case, his son's right to a similar exclusive use of that part of the fruit of his father's labour which the latter has given him must be a power which the son should have because its exercise by him is a condition of his father's really being able to do what he wishes with the fruits of his labour. So also the policeman's right to enter into a suspect's house, ultimately granted to him by the government, is a power which he should have because its exercise is the means to the good which consists in the maintenance of law and order. But this power is only a means to the good if it is exercised by a person who has been permitted to do so by the persons who alone have the right to grant this permission. Thus it is that certain rights, which a man possesses only because others have granted them to him, are yet powers which he ought to exercise only because his so doing is a means to the good. If their exercise were not a means to the good, then no one could possibly have the right to grant them to him.

Men have long spoken of natural rights, though they have done so less often than of natural law, and it is perhaps relevant to our inquiry to consider why they have felt the need to do so. There is no point in quarrelling about words, in insisting—as some critics have done—that it is improper to speak of *natural* rights on the ground that all rights are social. What matters to us therefore is to consider what they want to say about those rights which they call *natural*.

There has always been considerable confusion as to what exactly natural rights are supposed to be, but, nevertheless, it seems fair to presume that all persons who have asserted their existence have claimed that one or more of the three following propositions are true. Firstly, there exist certain rights which are unconditional and inalienable. Secondly, there are certain rights which men possess independently of the society in which they live. Thirdly, there exist rights which men ought to possess whether or not society, or rather any majority of its members, is of the opinion that they should. A consideration of these three propositions will suffice to clarify our attitude to the whole question of natural rights.

Let us take the first proposition first. Is it possible that there can exist any such thing as an unconditional right? It seems evident that it is not possible. Whether a man should or should not exercise a particular power under certain circumstances is always a possible matter of dispute. There may be certain powers the exercise of which is in itself good, which yet should not be secured to any one under the circumstances. So also there may exist other powers, whose exercise by certain persons is undoubtedly likely to promote some ultimate good, which yet should not be secured to them because their exercise of them would involve a more than equivalent curtailment of other men's powers, where their exercise of them is itself good. There is, then, no natural priority of either of these two main kinds of rights over the other. Nor yet is there any priority of them over what we have agreed to classify as a third kind of right, although it is, in fact, nothing more than a species of the second. Just as there is no action which is right under all circumstances, so also there is no unconditional right.

It has sometimes been alleged that there exists at least one unconditional right, namely, the right to consideration, which a man always possesses under all possible circumstances. But this so called unconditional right is nothing more than an assertion of the fact that the man is capable of rights. A man's rights must always be taken into consideration, but only because he possesses them. The rights which are considered are necessarily particular, and the consideration is merely an acknowledgement of the duty to respect them. When a man says, 'I have the right to be considered', he is saying that it is the duty of other men to respect any rights which he may have; he is not claiming a right which is independent of these others. It remains true, therefore, that there can exist no such thing as an unconditional right, since the ability to possess rights is not, strictly speaking, itself a right. It cannot be said that A's duty to secure B in the exercise of all his rights implies a general and unalterable right on B's part to the performance of this duty by A. A's duty to secure B in the exercise of all his rights is merely the sum of his duties to secure him in the exercise of each of them, so that it cannot imply any further right on B's part. Of course, if A is to perform his duties towards B adequately, he will continually have to ask himself what exactly the rights are which B possesses; that is to say, he will continually have to think of B as a creature who is capable of rights; but this will not be a further duty, but merely a means to the performance of the others.

We may now pass on to the second proposition, the one that asserts that men can possess rights quite independently of the fact of their being members of society. If we bear in mind the definition of rights which was offered at the beginning of this chapter, it becomes clear that a man living entirely apart from his fellows and never coming into contact with them cannot be a possessor of rights. He cannot be a possessor of them because there exist no powers which he is able to exercise and which the beings with whom he comes into contact ought to secure to him. Beasts and fishes, not being rational creatures, have no duties, so that it is not possible to have rights against them. It is only beings who have attained to a level of moral and intellectual development sufficient to enable them to understand what is meant by moral obligation who are capable of duties and against whom it is possible to have rights. It is not until he comes into contact with such beings as these that man, or any other creature, can become the possessor of rights.

There is, moreover, a further sense in which rights cannot be held outside society. It is probably true, as a statement of fact, that it is only within society that men can develop into rational and moral beings. If, then, no society exists, there exist no beings capable of the conception of duty and against whom it is possible to have rights. Men, of course, are not now in isolation and never have been, so far as we know, so that it is not possible for us to be certain that their being moral and rational is an effect of their life in society. But if we cannot have knowledge, we can express very probable opinions. When minds are in regular and intimate connexion with each other, the effect of this on all of them is so great that we can fairly assume that they owe practically all the higher qualities that they have to the fact that they are not isolated. If, then, we take it for granted that the statement that men could not be capable of duties outside society, though not self-evident, is yet very probably true in the sense that all available evidence points to that conclusion, we may suppose that the second of our propositions is also false.

There is, however, a sense of the word 'society' which is quite compatible with the truth of our second proposition. If society is taken to be the same thing as the State, then it no longer follows that no rights can be held outside it, since it is obviously not true that men could not be intelligent and moral beings outside the State. The State is no more than one organization amongst many, and it is clearly not a mere association of minds. It is a co-operation of minds with a view to the promotion of certain ends, and the difference between it and other organizations consists in a difference in the nature of the ends that it promotes and of the means to which it has recourse for their promotion.

There is another sense of the word 'society' which is again compatible with the existence of rights outside it. If by society is meant not a mere contact between rational beings, but a regular and intimate connexion between them, it then becomes possible for men to have rights outside society but not independently of it, since it was only their previous life within it which made them capable of duties. As soon as Man Friday came into contact with Robinson Crusoe he acquired rights against him, in spite of the fact that they were alone on the island and had never seen each other before. The German's early life in Hamburg had made him capable of having duties, so that it was possible for any living creature to acquire rights against him. On the other hand, supposing the society in which Friday had lived to have been insufficiently advanced to make a moral creature of him, then, in spite of his being in some sense a social animal, yet Crusoe had no rights against him. This, no doubt, constituted a superiority on the European's part and was one of the earlier instances of the white man's burden.

We have now considered the second proposition and have concluded that, although rights are never held independently of society, since it is in society alone that man becomes a moral creature, yet they may be held outside it, provided that the word 'society' is taken to mean something more than a mere contact between rational creatures, or between rational and irrational ones. We may now consider our third proposition, which asserts that there exist rights which men ought to possess whether or not society or any majority of its members are of the opinion that they should.

It seems that the truth of this third proposition is evident as soon as it is considered in the light of the above definition of rights. So long as the exercise of certain powers is good in itself or a means to the good, then, provided there exist rational beings against whom they can be held, these powers are rights whether or not any one is of the opinion that they are.

Certain philosophers have, however, argued that there can exist no such rights, and that the contract theorists who supposed that there could deduced their existence from a false premiss—the existence of a primitive state of nature in which men were supposed to possess certain inalienable rights by virtue of the natural laws which governed them in their relations with each other, even when none of them acknowledged obedience to any political superior. Locke, for instance, asserted that men living in this state of nature found it inconvenient, if not impossible, to coerce the recalcitrant into obedience to the laws of nature and of reason, and so bound themselves together by contract to set up an authority over them to which they would give up certain of their natural rights for the better securing of the rest.

We should gain nothing, for the purposes of this book, by entering into a criticism of Locke's account of the origin of the state or of the rights of which the individual was possessed before he bound himself to membership of a political society. We will say only that the truth of our third proposition does not in any way follow from that of Locke's account of the state of nature and of the origin of political society. Yet it was under cover of their attacks made upon this account that some of the major political thinkers of the last century also rejected certain of Locke's other contentions, which, in spite of various shortcomings in the manner of their elaboration, were and are substantially true. Having shown that there never existed a state of nature, they assumed that there could not exist such things as natural rights, but by natural they meant unrecognized rights. If, then, we accept their definition of natural, it at once becomes clear that no mere historical argument as to the probable origins of political society and of the moral intelligence in men can possibly suffice to disprove the existence of natural rights. The opinions of the majority of our fellow men are very important to us when we are discussing the question of what powers we can, in fact, exercise, but not when we are deciding which ones we ought to possess.

Since it is of the greatest importance to us, towards the establishing of the main argument of this book, to insist upon the existence of rights which do not owe their origin to their recognition by governments or by the general public, it will be necessary for us to consider in greater detail the main arguments advanced against them by their opponents. It will not be necessary to deal with the contentions of each opponent in turn, but merely to choose one or two of them who express themselves more clearly than the rest and who, for this reason, do not baffle criticism, since they can at least be understood. The two that come most readily to mind are Green and Ritchie, with whom it is occasionally possible to come to grips, as they are less prone than their fellows to hide their arguments behind an impenetrable fog of Hegelian phraseology.

Green defines a right as a 'power claimed and recognized as contributory to a common good',[1] and again as 'a power of which the exercise by the individual or by some body of men is recognised by society, either as itself directly essential to a common good, or as conferred by an authority of which the maintenance is recognised as so essential'.[2] He also tells us that 'No one has a right to resist a law or ordinance of government, on the ground that it requires him to do what he does not like, and that he has not agreed to submit to the authority from which it proceeds; and if no one person has such a right, no number of persons have it. If the common interest requires it, no right can be alleged against it. Neither can its enactment by popular vote enhance, nor the absence of such a vote diminish, its right to be obeyed.'[3] And finally, to make his point quite clear, we will quote him when he says: 'Rights are made by recognition. There is no right but thinking makes it so.'[4]

We are told, then, quite plainly, that rights are powers which men must have if they are to be able to promote something called the common good, and which they ought not to have unless their governors or the majority of their fellow men are of the opinion that they should have them. For the moment we will concentrate our attention on the *recognition* which is supposed to create rights. What actually does this *recognition* consist in? It is obvious that it consists in no more than the opinions of a number of people as to what powers a man should have. It is these opinions, then, that give that man his rights. But they are opinions about rights, and must therefore create their own objects. We are thus

---

[1] *Lectures on Political Obligation*, p. 110.
[2] Ibid., p. 113. [3] Ibid., p. 110. [4] Ibid., p. 140.

brought back once more to an argument similar to that of the subjectivists, who believed that the *esse* of objects of knowledge was *percipi*.

This belief, as is well known, is still widely favoured among philosophers in spite of the objections advanced against it. Moreover, it must be remembered that some philosophers, who once thought it self-evident that a thing must already exist in order to become the object of knowledge or opinion, no longer do so.

It is, of course, possible to hold that the *esse* of things is *percipi* without holding that knowledge creates its object. Colour cannot exist without shape, yet those who assert this do not confuse the relation between them with that between maker and made. But, for all this, the view seems not merely false, but absurd. In the first place it is not unlikely that the dictum *esse est percipi* is, when analysed, meaningless. In the second place, there seems no reason for believing that things cannot exist when not the objects of awareness. Moreover, even if there were any such reason, it would not suffice to make sense of the dictum in question.

But, however this may be, Green certainly does confuse knowing and making, for he says that there is no right but thinking makes it so.[1] No more is possible than to point out this confusion and to deny the contention which embodies it.

There is, of course, a sense in which rights are mind-dependent, in that it is only minds that can be subjects of rights. But most persons would agree that rights, though their existence depends upon that of minds, can be possessed by individuals who are not aware that they possess them. It is further agreed that they can possess them and ought to be able to exercise them, even though other people do not

---

[1] Persons who, for instance, hold that good means 'approved of' are not, of course, committed to the view that rights are made by recognition. There is nothing stated in this chapter to which they need object.

acknowledge that they ought. A negro slave, unable to understand what rights are, and supposed, by all the members of the society of white men amongst whom he lives, to possess none, is not for that reason incapable of them. Indeed, a creature need only be alive in order to be capable of rights, although it can only possess them against rational creatures, since they alone can have duties towards other animals. Vegetarians, amongst others, suppose that even a pig should be allowed to live out the full course of its natural life, in spite of the fact that its flesh provides a considerable part of the European's usual diet. Their contention, even if we consider man's right to eat pork to be superior to the pig's right to life, is not, on the face of it, an absurd one. We should not, for instance, deny the pig's right to life on the ground that it is not a rational creature. We can deny its right, and so refute the vegetarians, only by proving a superior right on man's part, or else by showing that man is not a rational animal, so that it is not possible for the pig to have a right against him. The view that animals can have rights may not recommend itself to every one, but it seems to follow logically from the definition of right offered at the beginning of this chapter as a power which a creature ought to have, in the sense of a power which rational creatures ought to secure to him. He ought to have it because rational creatures ought to secure it to him; and they ought to secure it to him because his having it would be either good in itself or else a means to what is good. The qualification 'in the sense of a power which rational creatures ought to secure to him' is brought in to make it clear that animals cannot have rights against non-rational creatures, since these latter are incapable of duties.

It may not be difficult for persons who suppose that animals cannot have rights to agree that men have them, either because their exercise of them is itself good or else a means to what is good. To say that anything ought to exist is the same thing as to say that rational creatures ought to promote its existence and also implies that its existence would be good. The statement 'A ought to exist' is elliptical. Since A does not exist, it is impossible that it should be its duty to do so. The bringing of A into existence is the duty of all rational creatures capable of the judgements 'A's existence would be good' and 'it is our duty to bring A into existence'. Now, if A is a power which could be possessed by a rational animal, circumstances being such that its possession of it would be good, it is the duty of that animal and of all other animals who are rational to bring A into existence. So also, if A is a power which could be possessed by an irrational animal, circumstances again being such as to make this possession good, it is the duty of all rational animals to bring A into existence, even if the future possessor of A is itself incapable of this duty.

A person might, of course, accept these arguments and still maintain that the lower animals cannot have rights. He might, for instance, claim that the exercise of a power by a lower animal can never be either good in itself nor yet a means to what is good. Such a claim would, however, appear to most people very much weaker than the claim that the lower animals cannot have rights. And yet, on our view, it would amount to pretty much the same thing. There may be even philosophers who think that they ought to go out for walks because it would give pleasure to their dogs if they went out with them. But if they do this, it is presumably because they think that their dogs' pleasures are also good, as well as their own, and should, therefore, be taken into account. If, then, it is not absurd to suppose that philosophers have duties towards dogs, neither can it be absurd to suppose that dogs have rights against philosophers, for to suppose the former is to imply the latter.[1]

This discussion of the rights of the lower animals should

[1] There seems to be a widespread prejudice against the view that animals can have rights. It is found even in Sir David Ross's book *The Right and the Good*, where it is argued that, though men may have duties towards animals, animals cannot have rights against men. This contention seems to be illogical.

make it clear in what sense it is true that rights are dependent upon the existence of minds. They are dependent upon their existence not because they are created by the mental activities of which they are the objects, but because they can be possessed only by creatures who have minds against creatures who not only have minds, but whose mental qualities are sufficiently developed to render them capable of duties. There should not arise any question of *recognition* so long as we are considering merely what powersmen or the lower animals should have. Such a question arises only when we come to discuss what powers they can, in effect, exercise, for no one will dispute that a strong belief entertained by a large majority of the members of any society will sometimes, however erroneous it may be, deprive men of powers which they ought to have. This, of course, is a matter of the greatest practical importance, for men are seldom so much injured in their rights as by the obstinate opinions of their neighbours. The theoretical case, none the less, cannot be upset by this consideration, for the necessary conditions of a man's exercising his rights are not the same as the conditions of his possessing them.[1]

It is significant that Green, although he often asserts that rights are made by recognition, also sees fit, in Chapter *A* of his *Lectures on Political Obligation*, to speak of 'a system of rights and obligations which should be maintained by law, whether it is so or not, and which may properly be called 'natural'; not in the sense in which the term 'natural' would imply that such a system did exist or could exist independently of force exercised by society over individuals, but 'natural' because necessary to the end which it is the vocation of human society to realize'.[2] He then goes on to 'dis-

---

[1] False political theories are not, perhaps, as dangerous to men's freedom as the passions of the selfish or prejudiced men who make use of them for their own purposes. But if they are not the causes of political injustice, they often provide excuses for it and so are not themselves as harmless as might appear.

[2] *Lectures on Political Obligation*, p. 33.

tinguish the system of rights actually maintained and obligations actually enforced by legal sanctions ("Recht" or "jus") from the system of relations and obligations which should be maintained by such sanctions ("Naturrecht"); and holds that those actions or omissions should be made obligations which, when made obligations, serve a moral end; (and) that this end is the ground or justification or rationale of legal obligation'.[1] These rights which are not maintained by the State are asserted to be 'natural', not because they are maintained by public opinion, but because they ought to be maintained by the state. Presumably there might exist *natural* rights in this sense, even if they were recognized neither by the government nor by the majority of the members of a society, so long as their exercise would tend to promote the existence of what is good. We also get the same view expressed by Ritchie when he talks to us of 'natural rights, those rights which ought to be recognized'.[2]

This mention of rights which ought to be recognized seems to imply that rights are not made by recognition. Green, therefore, either should not talk of natural rights at all, since by a natural right he can mean only an unrecognized power, which, by his own definition, cannot possibly be a right, or else should give up his definition. But, if he ceases to talk of natural rights and still retains his definition, he is left with certain unrecognized powers which should be recognized, but which yet are not rights.

Now, if these powers ought to be recognized it follows also that they ought to be possessed, for it is only because they ought to be possessed that they ought to be recognized. Moreover, if they ought to be possessed, it is clear that the possession of them would be either itself good or else a means to the good. In either case, their want of recognition, making it impossible for their potential possessors to exercise them, diminishes or, at least, prevents the increase

---

[1] Ibid., p. 38.
[2] *Natural Rights*, p. 99.

of what is good. It is clear, then, that this want of recognition is productive of evil, or else a hindrance to the good, in spite of the fact that no one is wronged, since no one is deprived of his rights. This paradoxical conclusion, at which we must necessarily arrive, if we start with the supposition that there exist powers which should be rights and yet are not, appears to be false.

It becomes further apparent, if this question is carefully considered, that a distinction of this kind between rights and powers which should be rights involves a misuse of ordinary language, for it then becomes possible to say that a man ought to be allowed to perform a certain action, although he has no right to perform it. This, of course, would not be a misuse of language if the word 'right' were here synonymous with the phrase 'legal right', but it is clear that any such interpretation of it would not be sanctioned by Green. Moreover, if a man ought to have a power, and if his fellows ought to recognize that he should have it, it is clearly his duty to exercise it, whether or not all, or any majority, of the persons with whom he comes into contact are of the opinion that he should. And yet, if we accept Green's definition, we are obliged once again to involve ourselves in a patent absurdity, for we must admit that there are actions which it is a man's duty, but not his right, to perform. Nor is this criticism unfair to Green, for these are conclusions at which we must necessarily arrive, if we start from the two assumptions that rights are made by recognition, and that there exist powers which are not, and yet should be, rights.

Green tells us not only that rights are made by recognition, but also that they are powers which men ought to have, if they are to be capable of contributing to the common good. This is made clear in the passage which runs— 'that I may have a life which I can call my own, I must not only be conscious of myself and of ends which I present to myself as mine; I must be able to reckon on a certain free-

dom of action and acquisition for the attainment of those
ends, and this can only be secured through a common recognition of this freedom on the part of each other by members
of a society as being for a common good. Without this, the
very consciousness of having ends of his own and a life
which he can direct in a certain way, a life of which he can
make something, would remain dormant in a man.'[1] Ritchie
concurs in this opinion when he tells us that 'the good of a
community gives us our only criterion for judging of what is
right for individuals to do; but the good of a community is
itself identical with the good of its members'.... 'The good
for man is always a common good'.[2] He also agrees that it
is because man, as an intellectual and moral being, is the
product of a life lived in constant contact with his fellows
that he can have no rights against 'society'. 'The person
with rights and duties is the product of a society, and the
rights of the individual must therefore be judged from the
point of view of society as a whole, and not the society
from the point of view of the individual.'[3]

In the last chapter we attempted to show that there could
not exist any such thing as a good which was common to
several persons at once, at least not in the sense required by
Green and others who think like him. It would not be wise
to add new arguments to the ones already elaborated, since
any such additions would certainly be less cogent than their
predecessors, so that persons not convinced by those which
have gone before would not be likely to think better of any
which might be added to them. No more need be said than
that, if no such common good exists, neither do any such
rights.

Any person, looking carefully into his own mind, will
readily convince himself of the tenacity of many of his false
opinions, and will be amazed at the ingenuity with which
they clothe themselves in new forms whenever reason makes

[1] *Lectures on Political Obligation*, p. 122.
[2] Ritchie, *Natural Rights*, p. 99.   [3] Ibid., p. 101.

an attack upon them. Confusion of thought is so natural to man that he will often persuade himself that his ideas are new for no better reason than that he uses new words to express them. It may be, therefore, that there are many people who would not allow that rights are made by recognition, but who would take no exception to Ritchie when he says that 'natural rights, those rights which ought to be recognized, must be judged entirely from the point of view of society'.[1]

What does Ritchie mean by 'the point of view of society'? Society, a number of human beings who live together, is not a mind, but an association of minds. It cannot, therefore, have a point of view. Ritchie's phrase must be taken to be no more than a shorter way of expressing what might be more fully expressed in the words 'the points of view (i.e. opinions) of all the persons (or of any majority of them) who, in so far as they come into fairly constant contact with each other, can be said to form a society'. But even this elucidation is misleading and does not suffice to make Ritchie's meaning clear. We still remain in doubt as to what the ideas are that he is failing to express by the words 'must be judged entirely from the point of view'. How, exactly, does one man set about *judging* a thing from the point of view of another? Moreover, in what is this judgement itself supposed to consist? From the context it would appear that *judging* a natural right consists in arriving at an opinion that a natural right either is or is not what it appears to be, i.e. a right which ought to be recognized. But the recognition of the right itself consists in the opinion that it is a right, so that it appears that Ritchie is telling us that we must arrive at the opinion (i.e. judge) that a right is a power about which an opinion that it is a right should be arrived at (i.e. a natural right), taking into consideration only the opinions about it of the persons who form a society with us (i.e. entirely from the point of view of society).

[1] Ritchie, *Natural Rights*, p. 101.

That is to say, in deciding whether certain powers which appear to be rights really are so, we must take nothing into consideration excepting only other persons' opinions that they are, or else are not, rights. And so we return once more to the view that rights are made by recognition.

It might be objected to this attempt to find out what Ritchie means by the extremely ambiguous sentence that has been quoted, that it does not take into account the possibility that the words 'from the point of view of society' may mean not 'taking into consideration the opinions of the persons who constitute the society' but 'taking into consideration the question of whether the power, if exercised, would tend to promote the "common good" of these same persons'. The phrase 'from the point of view of' is, in ordinary language, sometimes used as a synonym for 'according to the opinion of', and sometimes as equivalent to 'in the interests of'. Ritchie might just as well have meant the latter as the former, and it will not do to pretend to be certain which of the two he meant. There is interest only in pointing out that both views are wrong, since there can be no common good any more than there can be rights made by 'recognition'.

Many people are attracted to the theory that rights are made by *recognition* chiefly because they suppose that the general acceptance of it tends to promote law and order. They are fearful of the consequences of admitting that society (i.e. the majority of the members of society or the most powerful section in it) or else the government are not the final judges of whether certain powers should be exercised or not. There may be a great deal to be said for their fears, just as there may be much to be said for those who believe that the consequences of the opposite admission, that society and the government should be final judges in this matter, will be even more dangerous. Whether their fears are well grounded or not does not affect the present issue. The inquiry is into the nature of rights and not into the possible consequences of a general acceptance of any particular theory concerning them. True opinion may be dangerous, but it cannot be the less true for that reason.

Amongst the arguments which Ritchie brings forward to the support of his theory of rights is one which is based on the fallibility of conscience. The appeal from authority to Nature, he tells us, often takes the form of an appeal to conscience or to the individual's own reason. The authority of conscience is, of course, not less fallible than that of society and the government. There is, therefore, no reason for supposing that the individual is likely to be a particularly good judge of what powers he should be allowed to exercise.

This contention is undeniable, but it cannot be used as an argument in favour of the view that rights are made by recognition. One man's thinking that he has a right does not give him that right, any more than many men's thinking he had it would do so. Those who deny that rights are made by recognition make their denial absolute. They do not appeal to the conscience, for to do so would be the same as to assert that rights are made by recognition, so long only as the recognition is that of the man who claims the rights. The appeal to conscience would, in effect, be even more absurd than Ritchie's own appeal to society. His contention, therefore, though undeniable, is irrelevant. It does not strengthen his own position, which is none the less weak for his successful attack upon the still weaker position of the men, if any such exist, who out-Ritchie Ritchie.

The authority of conscience (i.e. of the individual's own reason in so far as it deals with questions of morality) is not ultimate in the sense of being infallible. Still less is it ultimate in the sense that a man's thinking it so makes an action right or a power a right. It is ultimate only in the sense that no free agent can possibly appeal to any other authority. The magistrate who obeys the orders of his superior is as much a responsible agent as the rioter who throws stones at him. Both have acted on their own authority, in the moral if not the legal sense of that word, since it was just as open to the magistrate to disobey his superior as to the rioter not to throw stones. Indeed, the man who concludes that he must always do what he is told must at least come to the original conclusion for himself. In deciding what he must do, he is no more capable of avoiding the ultimate authority of his own will and reason than is the anarchist who hates the government and despises his fellow creatures. In the case both of the magistrate and of the rioter, other men provide sanctions to increase the probability of both men's doing what these latter would like them to do. If the rioter insists upon throwing stones, his desire to do so must get the better of his desire to avoid imprisonment, or any other unpleasantness his fellow men have in store for him. So also the magistrate, if he wishes to leave the rioter in peace, must weigh the consequences of his action. He is liable to dismissal, or, what is sometimes worse, to the contempt and dislike of persons of the same social standing as himself. There is a restraint put upon his freedom just as much, but hardly more, than in the case of the rioter. Both of them are restrained from acting as they feel inclined, in so far as the fear of the consequences of so doing are likely to prevent them from throwing stones or from disobeying their superiors, as the case may be. None the less, whatever the restraints that are put in their way, they are still responsible agents so long as they are rational creatures capable of voluntary action.

The ultimate authority of men's will and reason as against the will of society, on which Ritchie pours scorn, is, therefore, ultimate, not on any grounds of perfection and infallibility, but for the very plain reason that it cannot be otherwise. The *will of society*, unless it means no more than the wills of many individuals, does not in fact exist, and cannot, therefore, be an ultimate authority for anything. The most shameless sycophant is, in this matter, in the same position as the Grand Monarch himself. Both are equally responsible for their actions, though the latter is more free in the sense of having fewer restraints put upon his actions by his fellow men. The opinion of Ritchie, that he has no rights except only such as the majority of his fellow men believe that he has, is itself a mental act for which he is responsible at the bar of common sense. For his opinion that the majority of his fellow men are the best judges in this matter is just as much personal and fallible as it would have been had it expressed the utmost contempt for them.

Before going on to a consideration of the problem which we have set ourselves in the next chapter we must give some account of the relation which exists between rights in general and what are usually called legal rights.

Legal rights, in the view here advocated, are no more than a special kind of rights of which it can just as truly be said as of any others that they are powers which men ought to exercise because their exercise is either good or a means to the good. They differ from rights which are not legal only because an acknowledged political superior is prepared to protect all persons living under his jurisdiction in their exercise of them. If this political superior is also willing to protect his subjects in their exercise of certain powers which they should not possess, the mere fact of his willingness does not convert these powers into rights. For instance, if it is wrong to kill one's fellow men, then no expressed intention on the part of a government to protect its subjects in their killing of foreigners can possibly give them the right to do so. If, in fact, they do so, they will not be committing murder, for murder means illegal killing, but they will be acting wrongly. No man can have a right to act wickedly or to promote evil, so that he can never have a right to empower others to do so.[1] He may, of course, have the power

---

[1] It is not intended to deny that legally protected powers to do wrong are often called rights. The word has more than one meaning, but only one is discussed in this chapter. The two classes of rights have many members in common.

to protect others in their evil and stupid actions, but that has nothing to do with the matter.

This does not mean that the government is not a creator of rights within certain limits. In so far as it has certain functions to perform, it may, in order to perform them properly, have to make certain regulations and to enforce obedience to them. These regulations will obviously place innumerable restraints upon the freedom of the persons who have to comply with them. They will greatly modify their powers and therefore also their rights, in that it will be true of many of their powers that they should exercise them only because their governors are of the opinion that they should. But the right to make regulations must first belong to the government before any of its legislative and administrative acts can, properly speaking, be said to modify, restrict, or multiply men's rights as apart from their mere powers. Moreover, this right to make regulations is itself a limited right, as Locke told us over two centuries ago, and as soon as the government begins to make regulations outside these limits, its actions, though respected by every court of law in the land, are not founded on right and should, therefore, be opposed by every one who thinks that more good than evil will come from opposition.

The opinion that governments have unlimited rights has been popular with European lawyers since the end of the middle ages. It is the view that finds very forcible expression in the Austinian definition of sovereignty. It also finds expression in the works of most of the political philosophers who have adopted some form of Rousseau's theory of the General Will. But, in spite of the very impressive support that it has received from so many quarters, it is not difficult to see that it is false. Its philosophical adherents we have attempted to deal with in our chapter on the General Will. For a criticism of Austin we can do no better than refer the reader to Appendix *A* of Sidgwick's *Elements of Politics*.

The conclusions that have been arrived at in this chapter

may be enumerated as follows. Rights, so far from being made by recognition, are nothing other than powers which ought to be secured to men or to other animals, because their exercise by them is either good or else a means to the good. They are not absolute, because there are no powers whose exercise is good or a means to the good under all possible circumstances. Finally, they are independent of minds, not in the sense that mindless substances can possess them, but in the sense that they are not made by the acts of knowledge and opinion of which they are sometimes the objects.

The power to act freely is nearly always claimed to be a right. Government by consent is often supposed to safeguard this power better than any other sort of government. We must, therefore, in our next three chapters endeavour to describe this power, to discover whether it is a right and whether it is really better safeguarded by democratic governments than by any other sort.

CHAPTER V

FREEDOM

THE following discussion of the nature of freedom will avoid altogether the old controversy between determinists and indeterminists. It will do so for two reasons: in the first place, because it is not at all unlikely that the controversy is a mere war of words, and, in the second place, because, even if it allows of real difference of opinion, it is not relevant to the inquiry which is the subject of this book.

This controversy has lasted so long that every one who claims to treat of freedom in a philosophical manner is expected to take part in it. It is, therefore, incumbent upon any one who refuses to do so to justify his refusal. This we will now proceed to do as shortly as we can.

In the first place it is clear that the dictum 'every event has a cause' is a good deal less simple than might appear at first sight. Constant succession and concomitance is never observed as between simple sense-data,[1] for we do not notice that red things are always silent, or always hard, or always smooth, or always sweet, &c. Constant succession, or concomitance, is, therefore, only observed as between complexes whose constituents are not always observed to be conjoined.

Moreover, an event is not a complex of sense-data, but rather a change within that complex. Its state before the change is not usually called the cause of its state after the change. It is the change which is itself called the effect of some other change.[2]

When we consider how exactly it is that one event is isolated from another we see that it is the order of the phenomena which we observe which determines our classification of our sense-experience into a world of events. Thus it is that a general proposition concerning events

---

[1] By simple sense-data are meant the smallest parts of a sense-field which we notice separately.

[2] This is why day is not supposed to be the cause of night.

cannot be the ground for any beliefs about the order of our sense-experience. Indeed, it is, to a large extent, in order to make the Causal Dictum true that we classify our experience into the particular events into which we do classify them.

This, of course, is not to deny that there is regularity and repetition in the order of our experiences. Unless this were so, the classification which makes the simple statement of the Causal Law possible would itself not be possible. But it is important to notice that the description of this primary regularity and repetition would be extremely complicated. And yet it, and not the ordinary, vague, simple dictum, must be the real law of necessary succession and concomitance, if any such exists. But it is surely too much for any philosopher to claim that this law, which, so far as we know, has never yet been correctly stated, is self-evident.

It is not at all clear that this description, even if correctly stated, could be anything more than a description for it is difficult to see how and where the notion of necessity comes in. Since it is not possible to see that it follows from the nature of a particular change within a complex that it should be accompanied, followed, or preceded by some other particular change, it seems incredible that it should be obvious that such a change must have some particular change in a given temporal relation with it. It is, of course, true that the causal law is claimed to be known *a priori*. But all other *a priori* laws are illustrated in particular examples of their operation, and it is through these illustrations that men come to know them.

Philosophers have been particularly anxious to safeguard the causal law in order not to endanger the sciences. Even writers like J. M. Keynes, who have substituted some other principle to take the place of the causal law, have thought this substitution necessary and for the same reason. M. Nicod talks of a determinism (which, however, need not be more than probable) as necessary to enable probable laws to be reached through the elimination of possible alternatives. But it is difficult to seé why all this is necessary. It is only required to make certain assumptions in order to make a mathematical calculation of chances possible.[1] No self-evident first principle is necessary, nor need probability be assumed to be an objective relation between actual and possible events. The nature of such a relation is extremely obscure, and no one has ever troubled to explain how it is made less obscure by the causal law or any other self-evident principle which takes its place. Besides, this account of probability seems to make opinion a species of knowledge, the knowledge of a certain type of fact.

That a single negative instance can invalidate an hypothesis has always been thought particularly fatal to persons who deny the existence of a self-evident first principle in which the possibility of induction is grounded. But, of course, if what persons are looking for, and expect to find, are constant conjunctions, it is obvious that a single negative instance must prove that the conjunction supposed constant is not so. But if X has accompanied A ninety-nine times out of a hundred, though we may refuse to talk of a causal relation between them, we still go on to expect them to accompany each other in the great majority of future instances. And, of course, our original search for constant conjunctions might itself be prompted by nothing more than the nature of our experience.

It is, in fact, only scientists who find the hypothesis *same event, same cause* particularly useful. In ordinary speech we often talk of an event as having different causes at different times. It is only after scientific assumptions are taken into account that we come to believe that these different *causes* have a common element which is the real cause of the event in question. No amount of scientific investigation can, however, prepare the mind to grasp the self-evidence of the causal law, if it could not do so beforehand. The scientist

---

[1] Nor is it at all clear what, if any, is the relation between the calculus of chances and the probabilities in which the philosopher is interested.

differs from the ordinary man merely in that his observations are much more thorough and much more accurate.

Of course, the unsophisticated man stoutly asserts that 'something cannot come out of nothing, so that everything must have a cause'. But, whereas it is not at all clear that he requires an event always to have the same cause, he does seem to require the former to be produced by the latter in some sense which makes the causal law something more than a necessity of succession or concomitance. It is this requirement of common sense that makes possible such questions as, 'How can the cause cause its effect, if it ceases to exist at the moment when the latter comes into existence?' Such questions seem to many philosophers to be absurd, though others treat them seriously and try to answer them in philosophical terms by theories insisting that the notion of causality is unintelligible apart from that of substance.

Now it is obviously not permissible, in a book of this kind, to go at all thoroughly into this question. The fore-going paragraphs are not intended as an attack upon the determinist position, their purpose being no more than to show that the whole controversy between determinists and indeterminists is either very obscure indeed and most of the ordinary arguments advanced much weaker than they appear, or that it is not properly a controversy at all, neither side having as yet stated their position in an intelligible and satisfactory manner. In either case, it is far wiser to ignore the matter altogether.

The wisdom of this decision is made all the more evident when it is observed that, supposing an intelligible and self-evident causal law to be accurately stated, it must apply to all events, whether physical or mental, and cannot allow of the exceptions required by the indeterminist. If it is asserted that it does not apply to all events, such an asser-tion must be justified. It can, however, be justified only by showing that it follows from the nature of a certain kind of events that they cannot[1] have causes. This no indeterminist has ever attempted to do, though all of them have insisted that, except for some acts of choice, all events, mental and physical, are determined.[2]

Moreover, the freedom of the indeterminist, if it exists, is not one in which the political philosopher can be interested, for either a man can choose between his motives or he cannot. If he can, then no one can prevent his doing so, for, since it is, *ex hypothesi*, an undetermined choice, it must of its very nature be beyond the reach of all influences. For, if it could be influenced, it could be determined, and, therefore, would not be free choice. But the freedom in which the writer on politics is interested is one which men claim as a right and which they suppose others should secure to them.

Now that arguments have been advanced in favour of avoiding altogether the interminable discussion between determinists and indeterminists, it is time to go on to the proper task of this chapter, which is to discover what it is that people ordinarily mean by the word freedom. Their definition or definitions of it will not, of course, be accepted at their face value. They will serve only as pegs on which to hang the discussion, in the hope that the analysis of them will help towards the establishment of an accurate definition of the phenomenon which they misdescribe. For though it is ordinary people who give words their meanings, it does not follow that they are able to define them.

The first popular and quite obviously false definition of freedom which must be considered is the one which makes it equivalent to the power to do what one wishes. It is the most common of all and also the least plausible, so that it is

---

[1] 'Cannot' is the word accuracy requires and not 'need not', for a cause is, by definition, a necessary antecedent or concomitant. Yet most indeterminists allow both of determined and undetermined choices.

[2] The other main objection to the indeterminist, that there would be no sense in calling a man's choice his if it were undetermined by his character, is invalid. Besides, it begs the question.

an excellent illustration of the extreme inaccuracy of ordinary definitions of the words most often used in everyday speech.

It is, of course, quite clear that all action is necessarily voluntary, since it is never possible for a man to do what he does not wish. Indeed, to do what one wishes is the same thing as to act, for an action which has no motive is inconceivable. If, for instance, *A* threatens to shoot *B* unless he raises his hands above his head, then *B*'s motive for doing what he is required, although it consists in the fear of what will happen to him if he does not (or rather in the effect of this fear, which is the desire to do what may ensure its not happening to him), is as much his motive as any other motive would be.

There are no qualitative differences between desires (except differences in the degrees of their intensity) of which we are normally aware. We usually distinguish them in terms of the difference between their objects. But any attempt to show that a man is acting voluntarily when his acts are motivated by certain desires, and involuntarily when they are motivated by others, involves the fallacy whereby differences in the object of the will are supposed to result from differences within the will. As was seen in the second chapter, this fallacy enabled the Hegelians to make a distinction between wishes which are real and others which only appear to be so. This distinction, however, is obviously untenable, so that, since there is no possibility of choice between motives, we must conclude that action is always from the strongest motive. This does not, however, mean that to decide and to be carried into action by the most pressing desire amount to exactly the same thing, for it may be true, for instance, that a man's judgement that he is about to act in a certain way is a necessary condition of his doing so and forms part of the activity called decision.

We must now pass on to a consideration of that definition of freedom which makes it equivalent to the power to do what one wishes without restraint by others. This is the most common of all definitions of it, and it is the one which, above all others, recommends itself to the unsophisticated. This does not mean that it is more likely to be accurate than any other, but merely that it must constantly be borne in mind if we are ultimately to arrive at a correct definition of any one kind of mental phenomenon which most men call freedom, or at correct definitions of two or more kinds of mental phenomena, all of which they call by that name. Our object, as we have often repeated, is to discover what most people mean by the word 'freedom', for it is they who give the word its meaning or meanings, so that, although they define it wrongly, it is a consideration of their definitions that is the most hopeful method of finding out what they really mean.

A man is commonly supposed to be restrained in his freedom whenever other men act in such a way as to prevent his performing an action which he originally intended to perform, either by making it impossible for him to do so or else by supplying him with a motive for abstaining from it. No one maintains that a restraint has been placed upon him when the action which he contemplates is one which it is impossible for him to perform quite independently of the actions of other human beings. If a man should wish to turn his wife into stone, he is more effectively prevented from doing so by his inability to bring about the necessary chemical changes than he is prevented from beating her by the fear of the legal or social consequences. So also a man who is prevented by a lion from taking a certain path in the jungle is not usually supposed to have been restrained in his freedom. For if freedom, in this sense, meant the unrestrained power to give effect to all our desires, we should have to acknowledge that restraints were constantly being placed upon it, not so much by the actions of our fellow men, as by the material universe itself. It is, however, clear that men seldom mean by freedom the unlimited power to

give effect to all their desires, although they sometimes
define it as if this were its usual meaning.

The distinction that has been made between hindrances
which are said to constitute restraints upon freedom and
those which do not is immediately justified as soon as we
remember that freedom, in the meaning of the word which
we are at present discussing, is usually claimed to be a right
(i.e. a power in the exercise of which its possessor ought to
be protected). Now, since a right held by one man implies
corresponding duties on the part of other men, and must
necessarily do so, it follows that it cannot be held against
inanimate objects and animals incapable of the conception
of duty. That is to say, since a man's freedom, in this sense,
is his right, it can only be restrained by intelligent and moral
creatures. These latter, of course, may use the lower
animals and inanimate objects as a means to the compulsion
of their fellows, but it does not follow from this that it is not
they, but their tools, who are responsible for the restraint.

Moreover, ordinary language refuses to allow that a man
can be restrained from doing what it is impossible for him
to do. In the case of the man who wishes to turn his wife
into stone, the unsophisticated would insist that it is precisely because it is impossible for him to give effect to his
desire that he cannot be restrained from doing so. On the
other hand, in the case of the man who desires to beat his
wife, it is because he is able to do so that it is necessary to
restrain him. The unsophisticated are not, perhaps, as
certain that this freedom, which is a right, cannot be restrained by the lower animals, but the arguments advanced
in the last paragraph should be sufficient to establish this
contention.

We have asserted that one man restrains another whenever he acts in such a way as to make it impossible for him
to perform the action which he originally intended, or
whenever he acts in such a way as to supply him with a
motive for refraining from it. He can, for instance, prevent

him from reading a certain book which he intended to read, either by taking it away from him and throwing it into the fire, or else by threatening to inform the police of his intention. In both cases the man whose freedom has been interfered with will have been restrained from doing what he originally intended, although in the one case it will have been made physically impossible for him to do it, whereas in the other he will have been supplied with a motive for refraining from the contemplated action. These restraints are, *ceteris paribus*, thought to be equally evil, because, in spite of the very different methods adopted in the two cases, they are equally interferences with the prospective agent's freedom.

It will, however, have been noticed that men do not regard all actions which a man performs with a view to causing to arise in another man's mind motives for acting otherwise than he originally intended as interferences with the latter's freedom. If a man acts in such a way as to prevent another from acting as he originally intended, not by making it impossible for him to do so, nor yet by providing him with a motive for not doing so, which consists, for instance, in the fear of what he or other men will do to him if he does do so, but rather by stimulating in him a desire to perform some other action which he comes to regard himself as more willing to perform, then he is not said to be putting a restraint upon his freedom. If *A* offers *B* a ticket to a theatre at which a play which *B* very much wishes to see is showing, his action can be said to prevent the latter from going to the cinema to which he originally intended to go that same evening, but it is not called a restraint upon *B*'s freedom. *B*, in accepting the ticket and giving up his projected visit to the cinema, does not admit that he is coerced, and most people agree with him, so that it cannot be said that he is unfree.

Now at this stage it may seem that the distinction between freedom, in the sense that we are now discussing, and the lack of it, will have to be made with respect to the nature of the desire from which a man acts, or, to put it more accurately, with respect to the nature of the object of his desire. If he performs action X instead of action Y, because he wishes others not to do to him what they threaten they will do unless he performs X, a restraint is said to have been placed upon him. If, on the other hand, he performs action X instead of action Y through his desire to obtain a promised reward, no restraint is said to have been put upon him. And yet, in both cases, others have acted so as to cause to arise in his mind a desire to act otherwise than he originally intended. The difference between the two cases, it may be argued, appears to be nothing more than the difference between the objects of the desires which have arisen in the agent's mind as effects of another man's action. In the one case he acts otherwise than he originally intended from a desire to avoid the consequences of not doing so; in the other, from the desire to obtain the promised reward.

If a distinction were made between freedom and restraint in terms of the differences between the objects of desire, this would not, of course, involve the fallacy of arguing from differences in the objects of the will to differences in the nature of the will itself. For freedom would be defined as consisting in action from certain motives and not others, and restraint as consisting in action from these other motives. Nothing need be said which involves the fallacy that men act voluntarily when they act from certain motives, and involuntarily when they act from others, nor need it be suggested that they are only desiring when their desires are rational, and merely appear to be doing so when they are not.

There are, however, two main objections to making the distinction between freedom and restraint turn upon differences in the nature of the objects of desire. The first objection is that men often call actions free, though they are the effects of desires whose objects are similar to ones which are the objects of actions which they call unfree. For instance, it appears that men would not call every action unfree which is performed from a desire to avoid certain consequences of its non-performance consisting in the effects of other men's actions. It may be that unless A performs action X, B will perform action Y, which A does not wish him to perform. In order to prevent B's performing Y, A performs X, and yet is not said to be unfree merely because he performed X in order to prevent B's performing Y.

It is not even true that A would be unfree if B informed A that he would only perform Y if he, A, failed to perform X. For A and B may have made a bargain together, one of the conditions of which was B's refraining from performing Y in the event of A's performing X. Now it is quite true that the parties to a bargain are often said to have deprived themselves of a certain part of their freedom, but it is quite clear that the word 'freedom' is being used in a meaning different from the one whose ordinary definition we are now analysing. For in this latter meaning it appears that most people would agree that if the bargain were freely made its conditions could not constitute restraints upon the parties to it; at least, not until one or other of them regretted the bargain, and fulfilled its conditions from a desire to avoid imprisonment or the contempt of his fellow men. As soon as this latter desire became operative in his mind, A or B would be called unfree, and the object of the desire would be to prevent other men (e.g. the police) from performing certain actions. It would, therefore, be similar in kind to the ultimate object (B's non-performance of Y) of A's desire to perform X; so that this very example gives us a case of a free action's becoming unfree as a result of a change in the actual object of the desire of which it is the effect, though the object is of the same kind and is always the prevention of others from acting in a certain way, in which they declare they will act unless the original action is performed.

The second objection to which we alluded is that a distinction between freedom and restraint, in terms of the natures of the objects of desire, would offer us no explanation of how it is that people make certain mistakes when they speak about freedom. For though we know that all actions are voluntary, yet we cannot deny that men do call actions done under restraint involuntary, and the fact that they do so must be taken into consideration. We know that there must be some cause of so universal, though misleading, a manner of speaking, in which philosophers indulge, when not philosophizing,[1] just as readily as any one else. But mere differences in the natures of the objects of desire do not provide us with a clue as to why we all naturally adopt this misleading manner of speaking, and it is, after all, likely that a correct definition of freedom, in the meaning we are at present analysing, would give us such a clue. It need not, of course, do so. Certain misleading forms of speech have come into general use as a result of historical accidents. The correct form might provide us with no clue as to why the misleading form is used. Historical research might alone enable us to solve this problem. But when such a misleading form is found in almost every language, it is reasonable to suppose that there is something in the nature of the phenomenon which it misdescribes which makes this misdescription *natural*, in the sense of one which we might expect people to make.

This universal belief that unfree actions are somehow involuntary, though they are obviously not reflexes, and that they are done *against the wills* of their performers, is so interesting that it must be considered in greater detail. For, though it is false, the fact remains that it seems to unsophisticated persons to be a proper description of their experiences. We know, for instance, that if *A* threatens to shoot *B* unless he signs a certain paper, *B* supposes that he is being obliged to do what he does not wish to do. For

---

[1] This qualification does not apply to Hegelians, who have based their whole philosophy on a number of assumptions which, when analysed, appear to be everyday metaphors treated as if they were not metaphors but were accurate descriptions of reality.

some reason or other he refuses to allow that he is acting willingly when the motive from which he acts consists in the fear of what would be done to him by A did he not do what the latter requires of him. Were A's method of persuasion to consist, not in the threat of instant death, but in the offer of a large pecuniary reward, B would no longer consider himself the victim of coercion, but would maintain, should he act as A desired him, that he was doing what he wished to do. And yet it is obvious that in both cases the motive from which B is acting is known by him to have arisen in his mind as a direct result of an action on the part of A. To use a Kantian phrase, it is clear to B that in both cases A is treating him as a means only and not also as an end. But, for all that, he stubbornly insists that the two cases are quite different in kind.

If B were asked to explain in what it was that the difference between the two cases consisted, he would probably tell us that in the case of the threat he did not choose to act as A wished, whereas he did so in the case of the promise of a reward. He would make the difference turn not upon the quality of the motive from which he acted, nor yet upon the manner in which A caused it to arise in his mind, but upon the question of choice. He would, of course, allow that the manner in which A caused a desire to arise in his mind was all-important in determining whether or not he would be able to act as he chose, but it would be upon the choice or the lack of it, and not upon the way A acted towards him, that he would insist in making it clear that his action was free or otherwise. A, from his point of view, might imagine that he was using B as a means only and not also as an end, both when he threatened to shoot him and when he offered him a large sum of money, and it might be quite obvious to B that that was all that A was doing. But this, B would insist, could not alter the fact that he was being used as a means against his will in the first instance and with his consent in the second.

It seems, then, that *B*, when he maintains that he is free, is under the impression that he is able to choose between his motives, and that he is coerced only when he is prevented from acting, or when another's action prevents his choosing between his motives and obliges him to act from the one which arose in his mind as the result of this other's action. But there is no reason to believe that such choice is possible in any sense of the word which would not make a coerced action just as much an act of choice. Indeed, it is very difficult, if not impossible, to attach any meaning to the phrase 'a choice between motives' if it implies that this is a special kind of choice differing from all others. Experience does not reveal its existence to many philosophers (that is to say, persons whose business it is to reflect on these matters), though they are supposed to be as capable of it as any one else. On the contrary, the wider and the more accurate experience becomes, the more it increases men's belief in constant successions and concomitances.[1] Whether this order or regularity is necessary or not, it still deserves the name of determinism. The problem, therefore, if the nature of freedom is to be discovered, is to find some explanation of this phenomenon, called a choice between motives, which is compatible with determinism on the one hand and with the ordinary distinction between free and unfree actions on the other. In this way the limits of our problem are defined by everyday language, though its solution is not to be found within its scope.

[1] Of course, this does not apply to the thinkers usually called determinists, since they claim to apprehend *a priori* the universal validity of a law of necessary conjunction. But it does apply to those who claim merely to believe, however intensely, in the future continuance of these constant conjunctions. They avoid the word necessity altogether, but can still be said to believe in determinism, so long as that word is not used to mean *necessary* conjunction. It has been so used in the past, but it might, perhaps, in the present state of philosophical studies, be more convenient to alter its meaning. From now onwards in the chapter the word determinism will not be used in a sense which implies a belief in necessary succession. This, however, does not bind the user to the assertion that there is no law of necessary conjunction. On the other hand, it allows him to admit that there may be both uniformities and accidents. The definition of freedom which will be offered will not imply the existence of the latter.

The first definition of choice which is compatible with determinism, and which gives some promise of leading us to a plausible explanation of *B*'s distinction between freedom and coercion, is the one given by Stout in the essay on 'Voluntary Action' in his *Studies in Philosophy and Psychology*. In this he maintains that the phenomenon of choice or decision consists in nothing other than the prospective agent's awareness that he is about to act in a certain way and in the statement 'I will act in this way' which expresses this awareness. Decision or choice therefore consists, according to this theory, not in the fact of one motive's victory over all the others, but in the subject's awareness of the victory and the statement in which he expresses his belief about how he will act. This latter statement need not, of course, be uttered in words or openly expressed in any other way.

Stout asks, 'How does a desire differ from a volition?' and he answers:

'A volition is a desire qualified and defined by the judgement that, so far as in us lies, we shall bring about the existence of the desired end. . . . The desire is defined in this idea [of an end] together with the problematic judgement that we may or may not attempt to realise it. A volition, on the other hand, is a desire defined in the judgement that we are going to realise an end, if possible.'[1]

This account is an ingenious attempt to explain in what the phenomenon usually called decision or choice consists in a world which is entirely subject to law. Choice, in the ordinary definition of that word, cannot possibly exist; but there still remains to be explained how men come to believe that it does. Stout does not attempt this latter explanation, but he does attempt to find out what choice consists in, if its ordinary definition is taken to be incorrect. He proceeds by the only possible method, an analysis of what goes on in the mind when the alleged phenomenon of choice occurs. But, though it is clear that Stout's method is the correct one, it is

[1] G. F. Stout, *Studies in Philosophy and Psychology*, p. 53 (London, 1930).

not possible to use his conclusion as a criterion to distinguish between freedom and coercion.

Reflection on our own experience should convince us that, if what is usually called choice is to provide us with the criterion which we need, it cannot consist in the judgement or statement that a certain motive is about to bear fruit in action. In the case which we have already taken, when *A* threatens to shoot *B* if he does not sign a certain paper, *B* may be perfectly aware that the motive which consists in the desire to preserve his life is about to bear fruit in action, and this awareness may be expressed in his statement 'I will sign this paper', but it does not follow that he will allow that he chooses to act as he does. Moreover, it is because we believe that he is justified in his refusal to admit that he chose to sign the paper, that we approve the law when it does not hold him responsible for his action. The choice or decision, as ordinary language sometimes has it, did not rest with *B*, because he was forced to act 'against his will'.

It is true that ordinary language does sometimes speak of a man as being forced to make a decision which he does not wish to make. We sometimes hear such statements as 'I was compelled to come to this decision' or 'I was forced to choose this rather than that'. Now it is obvious that choice or decision, in this sense, cannot be the basis of a distinction between freedom and restraint, though it may very well conform to Stout's definition. The fact, however, still remains that there is an ordinary use of the word 'choice' which does make it the basis of this distinction, and which it is our purpose to discover.

Moreover, even Stout is not satisfied with his definition as it stands and takes care to amend it. He insists that he does not consider the statement 'I will act in such-and-such a way' as sufficient to constitute decision. When he discusses the case of the soldier who sneezes involuntarily and yet judges that he is about to sneeze, he tells us that

'there is a very important distinction to be made. A voluntary act is one which takes place in consequence of the judgement that, so far as in us lies, we shall perform it. The converse is not true. The act is not voluntary when the judgement that the action is going to take place arises because the action is already otherwise determined. In the present instance, the knowledge that the reflex impulse is triumphing, or is about to triumph, is not the condition which causes it to triumph.'[1]

This distinction may explain one of the differences between a reflex action, which is strictly speaking motiveless, and an action proper, but it does not provide us with a basis for differentiating between coerced and free action. It may be that the judgement 'I will sign this paper' is as much a condition of a certain desire's having effect in coerced action as the judgement 'I will go to the theatre' is a condition of a man's voluntarily going there. But this does not prevent ordinary language from often insisting that the first is not a proper case of choice or decision, whereas it never denies that title to the second.

Moreover, it is doubtful whether the statement 'I will do this' is itself a condition of a man's acting in the manner Stout has just defined. The statement, so far from being itself a part-cause of the triumph of a certain motive, may be no more than one of its effects. It, or rather the cognition which it expresses, may itself often be the condition of the disappearance of all or most of the motives likely to oppose the one which ultimately proves the strongest, and so explains how it is that Stout comes to think that it is a necessary condition of voluntary action. It may be a psychological fact that the knowledge that he is about to perform a certain action often destroys in a man all desires opposed to this performance. However this may be, and whether or not it suggested Stout's definition to him, the fact remains that decision or choice, as he conceives it, does not give us the criterion of freedom which we require. Nor does it even constitute, as he seems to imply, the most important difference

---

[1] Stout, *Studies in Philosophy and Psychology*, p. 59.

between voluntary and reflex actions, or rather, as some would prefer, between actions and reflexes. This surely consists in the fact that the former have motives or desires for their causes, whereas the latter have not.

We have already discussed some of the more usual definitions of freedom and have analysed the most common of all erroneous beliefs as to its nature. It is now time for us to attempt our own definition or definitions of it, which we believe will include within their scope all actions which men normally call free, and of which they say that they acted as they chose.

It seems that freedom must be defined, in its primary, though not necessarily widest, meaning, as action from a motive from which a man desires to act, or, at least, does not desire not to act, and the lack of freedom as action from a motive from which he does not desire to act. This definition, therefore, turns on the undoubted fact that men can and do desire to act from certain of their motives and not from others. For there are, clearly, readily analysable conative situations which can be defined as cases of unfree action, wherein men, though they are doing what they wish, are yet acting from motives from which they do not desire to act.

Now it is clear that freedom in this sense must be differentiated from freedom from constraint by others. For a man might very well be acting from a motive from which he did not desire to act and yet not be acting under constraint. So that freedom, in the sense of the absence of constraint by others, has a wider meaning than freedom as it was described in the previous paragraph. It should, however, be observed that this definition of freedom is positive, whereas freedom from constraint is negatively defined as consisting of all actions other than those done under constraint. This is the justification for considering this definition to be the primary one, and a little thought will make it clear that the wider freedom is defined as other than *a certain species* of unfree actions, in this meaning of the word unfree. For an action done under constraint is merely an action done from a motive from which a man does not wish to act, under circumstances such that this motive is the effect in his mind of other men's actions done with a view to this particular effect. That is to say that, since not all unfree actions are constrained, though all constrained ones are unfree, it follows that if the word 'freedom' is also defined as absence of constraint it acquires a wider, though necessarily secondary and derivative, meaning.

With regard to the freedom which is defined as unconstrained action, it is not altogether clear that most men would consider all actions from undesired motives, which are the effects of other men's actions consciously performed in order to bring them into existence, to be constrained. For the case of temptation must also be taken into account. Let us suppose that a man believes that the drinking of alcoholic liquor is a vice, but that he is, at the same time, inordinately fond of it. Can he, then, be said to be constrained by another man who places a glass of whisky in front of him when he is feeling particularly thirsty, so that he puts aside his good resolutions and drinks it? It appears that men's opinions are divided on this question. Sometimes they speak as if a man who yields to temptation were unfree, at others as if this fact, though it might increase their sympathy for him, did not entail any loss of freedom on his part. We may therefore conclude that freedom, in the sense of absence of constraint, is used in two meanings. In the former it means action from a motive other than an undesired motive which is the effect of other men's actions done with a view to this effect. In the latter it means all this with the further qualification that the undesired motive must consist in a desire to avoid threatened painful consequences, or else consequences the thought of which is painful. This very last qualification is put in so that the second definition may include cases of men threatening their victims with painless death,[1] the thought of which is alone painful. Of course, the thought of death, under the particular circumstances envisaged by the supposed constrainer and his victim, may not be painful to the latter. When this is so, it cannot, according to this second definition, constitute a real case of constraint. A promise to kill a man can under certain circumstances amount to a promise of a reward, but it then ceases to be a threat.

Of these two meanings of freedom from constraint, the second is considerably the more common. It has a further peculiarity which distinguishes it from the first, in that such constraint alone is usually accompanied by the emotion called fear. This emotion is not a desire, and is therefore never, strictly speaking, a motive for action, though it may, of course, be the immediate cause of unwilled movements of the human body. When it is said that the fear of anything is a motive for action, the statement is necessarily either erroneous or elliptical, in which case it is merely a convenient way of saying that the action is done from a desire which exists in the mind simultaneously with fear, and which may be its immediate psychological effect. But it must be insisted that the desire, however intense, to avoid anything is not the same thing as the fear of it, though it is very often the effect of fear.

These three definitions of freedom cover all actions which men, other than philosophers in the actual exercise of their trade, ever call free. It will be seen that the two secondary forms of freedom are not species of the primary, but that the narrower secondary is a species of the wider. On the other hand, the secondary forms are related to the primary, in that they are negatively defined as covering all actions other than those constituting instances of certain species of unfree actions, in the primary meaning of the word unfree. If, then, unfree actions, in the two secondary

---

[1] Death, it may be objected, can be neither pleasant nor painful. This is, of course, true, but its immediate physical causes may be.

meanings of 'unfree', are species of unfree actions in the primary meaning of that word, it follows that the two secondary meanings of freedom, though only derivative, are nevertheless wider than the primary.

We should like, at this stage, for our own and the reader's benefit, to invent a number of phrases which will enable us to refer more conveniently to the various sorts of motives and the different meanings of freedom which we have attempted to distinguish. Motives from which men desire to act we will call desired motives; motives from which they neither desire to act nor yet desire not to act we will call neutral motives; whereas motives from which they desire not to act we will call undesired motives. Freedom, in its primary meaning, can therefore be defined as action from a desired or a neutral motive, and the lack of freedom as action from an undesired motive. Freedom in its wider secondary meaning we will call freedom from restraint, and it will be defined as action from a motive other than an undesired motive which is the effect in the agent's mind of another man's, or other men's, actions done with a view to this effect. Freedom, in its narrower secondary meaning, we shall call freedom from coercion, and we shall define it as action from a motive other than an undesired motive which is the effect in the agent's mind of another man's, or other men's, actions done with a view to this effect, and consists in a desire to avoid threatened consequences which are either painful themselves or else the thought of which is painful.

Any one who accepts the above definition of freedom in its primary meaning will have no difficulty in accepting the two secondary definitions, so that we will confine ourselves to putting forward arguments in support of the former. Apart from the claim that it covers all actions which men frequently call free (which claim can only be tested by taking a fairly large number of instances and seeing whether the definition applies to them all), it is claimed for it that it affords an explanation of how men come to make certain erroneous statements which they quite often make when talking about freedom.

When men act from undesired motives they say that they are acting 'against their wills', because they are, in fact, acting from motives which they wish did not exist in their minds. It is, therefore, not unnatural that, not troubling to analyse these situations properly, they should assert that they are doing what they do not wish to do. Of course, whenever there is a conflict between motives there is not necessarily action from an undesired motive, for it may be that none of the defeated motives is a desire not to act from the victorious one, for they may be desires to realize objects other than the object of the victorious desire. If such is the case, the situation is not of the kind that results in action which a man usually describes as being done against his will.

This same characteristic of unfree actions, which explains how it is that men come to say of them that they perform them 'against their wills', also explains why they say of them that they do not choose to perform them. In these cases the word 'choice' is always used in one of its proper meanings, for to act as one chooses is to act freely. But, just as there are three meanings of freedom, so there are also at least three of choice, for the two words are, in these cases, synonymous.[1] And so, in this way, the primary definition acquires its justification. For it was insisted all along that our purpose was to discover what ordinary men mean by the word 'freedom', and that their definitions of it, although there might be cause to reject them, should always be regarded as valuable clues.

Another small advantage of the definition we offer is

[1] The word 'choice' has other meanings irrelevant to this inquiry. To act as one chooses sometimes means to act voluntarily, i.e. to act. At other times it means to be carried into action partly by desires which have arisen in the mind as the result of comparing the possible consequences of the realization of alternative objects of desire.

that it enables one to provide even the Hegelians with a slender excuse for some of their less astonishing statements about freedom. They tell us, for instance, that action from evil motives is not free. Now it is clear that most men disapprove of evil actions, for otherwise they would hardly call them evil,[1] so that most men desire not to act from evil motives. This does not mean, of course, that they do not desire to act from motives which are in fact evil, on the occasions when they do act from them, for on such occasions they usually persuade themselves that their motives are good, but merely that they would, if challenged, insist that they much preferred acting from good motives to acting from evil ones. This general preference explains why it is that men are so anxious to persuade themselves that they are acting from good motives, even when every one else is under the impression that they are not. It also explains why they are so anxious, when they find no practical alternative but to admit that they have been vicious, to disclaim responsibility for their actions by asserting that 'they have not been quite themselves'. This self-contradictory statement is often accepted as a sufficient excuse, probably because it is evidence of the sinner's preference for virtue over vice, which also often leads him to blame the Devil for his own misdeeds. On the other hand, only saints and exceptionally religious persons declare that God, rather than themselves, is responsible for their good actions.

Now the Hegelians, observing that men did not desire to act from evil motives unless they could persuade themselves that they were good, inferred that men only desired to act from good motives and never from evil ones, from which they went on to argue that men are free only when they are good. Their first inference is fallacious, since men obviously do often wish to act from evil motives, even if they usually

---

[1] This, of course, is not to imply that to call a thing evil is to say that most men disapprove of it, but merely that men do not usually call things evil unless they also disapprove of them.

take care to persuade themselves that they are good, so that there is no argument from a man's preference for good motives in general over evil ones to his not wishing to act from an evil motive on any particular occasion. But on our definition of freedom their second inference is correct, for if it were true that men never wish to act from evil motives it would necessarily follow that all evil actions are unfree.

The worst fault of the Hegelians, so far as their moral theory was concerned,[1] was that, though they continually complained about the inadequacy of ordinary definitions and conventional expressions, they nearly always accepted them at their face value and insisted upon asserting that they are literally true. When a man said to himself, after performing some vicious action or some action which he supposed to be vicious, that he was not 'really himself' when he performed it, they insisted that he must not use the phrase for its soothing qualities, but must accept it as an accurate description of a real situation. The inadequacy of such a phrase, they were anxious to maintain, consists in its metaphorical use. Taken literally it becomes the basic principle of ethics, the understanding of which is the open-sesame to that entire branch of philosophy.

These same metaphors puzzled the ancient Greeks and led them to make certain assertions not altogether different from those of Hegel and his followers. Thinking, however, that discretion was the better part of valour, they refrained from attempting to build up a complete theory of morals on these foundations. They contented themselves with suggesting that they must be understood to be more than metaphors, since they were keys to important truths which might otherwise escape notice. Virtue, they insisted, is proper to man, so that a vicious person is something the less a man for his vice. But to define an organism as pursuing certain ends does not justify us in supposing that it is any

---

[1] But this fault is also to be found in the other branches of their philosophy, though to a lesser extent.

the less that same organism when it does not realize those ends. And, *a fortiori*, if the organism is defined in respect of ends which it *ought* to realize, its failure to realize them cannot change its nature. For if it is true that man is an animal which ought to desire virtue it is also true that many men act viciously and are none the less men for doing so. On the contrary, it is only creatures capable of virtue who can be vicious.

When an organized being is defined as pursuing certain ends, then anything which does not pursue those ends cannot fall under the definition, but its mere failure to realize them would not, of itself, prevent its doing so. On the other hand, if that being is defined in respect of ends which it *ought* to pursue, then the mere fact that anything does not pursue these ends is not sufficient to prevent its falling under that definition, for it may still be truly said of it that it ought to pursue them. If, then, the statement 'Virtue is proper to man' is taken to mean that no animal can be a man unless it can truly be said of it that it ought to be virtuous, it may be permissible that this latter fact should form part of the definition of man. If, on the other hand, it is taken to mean that no animal is a man unless it always desires to be virtuous, it is obviously false, since many animals are called men even when they do not desire to be virtuous.

The definition of anything with respect to the ends it ought to pursue is likely to lead to misunderstanding. Men are less used to such definitions than to those which describe the sensible qualities of the things defined. If man is spoken of as an animal who ought to be virtuous, men will come to believe that some one who is not virtuous is 'less of a man' than some one who is. The same sort of misunderstanding occurs as a result of defining something with respect to one of its *powers*. Thus, if man is defined as a rational animal, it will be supposed by many that some one who reasons more often than his neighbour is 'by so much the more a man'. In this way men convince themselves that they are somehow not men when they are not acting as they alone of all animals can act, or as they alone of all animals ought to act. But it is clear that this conviction has no rational foundation. An isosceles triangle is not supposed to cease being isosceles by reason of those of its qualities which it shares with equilateral and scalene triangles, though it is distinguished from them by reason of those which it does not share with them. That the qualities in question should be powers makes no difference. A man is no less a man for being irrational, though he must be capable of reasoning if he is to be a man.

These considerations will, it is hoped, incline the reader to a favourable opinion of our primary definition of freedom, as well as of the secondary definitions derived from it, for the three between them cover nearly all actions which men ordinarily call free, and also provide us with a number of explanations and excuses, both for the linguistic practices of such men and the absurdities of philosophers. It now remains for us, in the next chapter, to consider these kinds of freedom and to determine whether they are all, or only some of them, good or a means to the good, and, if they are all good, whether they are equally so, or else each of them in a different degree.

CHAPTER VI

THE VALUE OF FREEDOM

WHENEVER there is a dispute as to whether any-thing possesses a certain property or not, it can be brought to a conclusion satisfactory to all parties only by one of them convincing the others that this thing is a member of a class of things which either do or do not possess this property. No conclusion is possible unless they can all be persuaded that the thing in question is a member of this class, and unless they agree that all the things which are members of this class do, in fact, or else do not, possess this property. That is to say, the only way to prove that A is or is not C is to point out that it is B, which either neces-sitates its being C or else excludes that possibility.[1] The things called A may constitute all the members of the class of things which are B, or alternatively they may constitute a mere species of a genus.

Our task, in so far as it is to be in the nature of a proof, must take the form of establishing that free actions are either members of a class of things which are good or else members of a class of things which are means to what is universally acknowledged to be good. If we find that proof is impossible, we will have recourse to mere assertion, being unable to do more than declare that free actions are good, and that ordinary men, in their everyday language and in their normal activities, obviously talk and act as if they believed they were good.[2] This last procedure would not

[1] The excuse for making these simple and obvious remarks is the curious belief entertained by some persons that disputes about moral questions are not properly disputes about objective matters, because the disputants, when they disagree, say, about the goodness of anything, do no more than attempt to point out that it is, or is not, the sort of thing which they all agree to call good. But the form of disputes about morals would be the same whether goodness were an objective quality of things or merely a subjective feeling towards them.

[2] They talk and act as if goodness were an objective quality, and not merely as if they approved of certain things and not of others.

amount to proof, for it would not proceed from agreed premisses to a necessary conclusion, but it would provide evidence in favour of the contention that free actions are good, which might incline persons who did not directly apprehend its truth to admit that it was at least probably true.

The first argument that comes to the mind of any one anxious to prove that freedom is good is suggested to him by the ordinary form of language which substitutes the words 'I did as I pleased' for 'I acted freely'. If free actions are themselves pleasant or are usually accompanied by pleasant emotions and unfree ones are unpleasant or accompanied by unpleasant emotions, then, since pleasure is good, freedom must be either good or else a means to what is good. For it is either a species of the genus of pleasant things or else it is a means to the existence of such a species.

The obvious objection to this argument is that all free actions are not pleasant, however true it may be that most unfree ones are unpleasant. For instance, a man who risks his life to save his friend is not performing a pleasurable action. He may experience pleasure at his friend's safety, which is itself the result of his action, but not necessarily the object of his desire. So also the pleasure which he gets from the successful setting aside of temptation does not usually form any part of the motive for resistance to it, nor yet prevent this latter from being a very difficult and unpleasant process.

This objection may be surmounted by the contention that, though all free actions are not, on the whole, pleasant, they may be pleasant by reason of their freedom; and, conversely, that, though many unfree actions may, on the whole, involve more pleasure than pain, they may yet be unpleasant by reason of their lack of freedom. That is to say, all free actions may necessarily involve some pleasure and all unfree ones some pain; so that, there being no other pleasure or pain to take into consideration as being specially connected with the free and unfree nature of actions as such, there arises a justification and explanation for the translation of the words 'I acted freely' into 'I did as I pleased', and 'I did not act freely' into 'I did not act as I pleased'.

It has been suggested by Professor Broad[1] that pleasure and pain are not themselves feelings, but are relational properties which feelings acquire according as their subjects desire to be rid of them or not. Thus an unpleasant feeling is one of which a man desires to be rid, a pleasant feeling one of which he does not desire to be rid. Broad makes it clear that he supposes their pleasantness or unpleasantness to consist directly in the fact that they are desired or not, and not in any further feelings which are themselves the effects of these desires. When we suffer a pain we have not two separate objects of consciousness, the feeling and its painfulness, but only one, which we describe as a painful feeling. Indeed, Broad contends that the same feeling may at one time be pleasant and at another painful, and yet it may be, on both occasions, a feeling of exactly the same kind.

If we treat desires as a species of feelings, we may apply Broad's theory to our account of freedom. We may maintain that actions from desired motives are good because they are necessarily also actions from pleasant motives, whilst actions from undesired motives are evil because they are necessarily actions from unpleasant motives. This leaves us with three kinds of actions differentiated in terms of good and evil: unfree actions, all of which are evil, and free actions, which are good or indifferent according as they are done from desired or neutral motives. So that, though all free actions are not good, yet they should, there being no other relevant considerations, always be preferred to unfree ones, since these latter necessarily involve a certain element of evil.

---

[1] C. D. Broad, *Perception, Physics and Reality*.

If we differentiate between primary and secondary[1] desires, on the ground that the latter always have the former for their objects, whereas the objects of the former are not desires, we may say that a free action, which is good in respect of its freedom, occurs whenever the continued existence of the primary desire of which it is the effect is the object of the strongest secondary desire. An unfree action occurs whenever the annihilation of the victorious primary desire is the unrealized object of the strongest secondary desire. Free, but indifferent, actions occur whenever primary desires are not the objects of secondary desires, or when two or more primary desires, of which one is victorious, are the objects of secondary desires of equal intensity.

It might be objected to this argument that, since the object of every desire is its own satisfaction, which can be called a feeling, every action must, on this view, be pleasant, whether it is free or unfree. For the desire which takes effect in unfree action must necessarily be stronger than the secondary desire, which would be satisfied by its annihilation, so that unfree action as such necessarily involves a balance of pleasure, without there being any need to take into account the special circumstances of any particular case. And though it may be true that every unfree action involves a certain amount of pain, yet since it necessarily involves a balance of pleasure there is no point in saying that when a man acts unfreely he is not doing what he pleases. Free actions may therefore be, on the whole, pleasanter than unfree ones, but both are pleasant, and therefore both are good in so far as pleasure is alone considered. And it must be remembered that on this view pleasure is precisely the good which actions, in respect of their freedom and unfreedom, tend to promote, though in different degrees.

[1] Tertiary desires and desires of an even remoter order can occur, but they need not be considered separately, since, *mutatis mutandis*, what is true of secondary desires will also be true of them.

This objection, which amounts to saying that, on the definition of pleasure which we have been discussing, there is no point in talking about acting as one pleases and as one does not please, since all actions are necessarily pleasant, gains further force when it is pointed out that it is not at all unlikely that unfree actions will be often more pleasant than free ones. For if, in the case of an unfree action, the victorious desire is very intense, and is fairly weak in the case of a free one, it may very well be that the unfree action will be considerably more pleasant than the free one. And it must be observed that, for instance, victorious desires in cases of coerced actions are apt to be very intense. Indeed, since most men are cowardly and timid, they probably form a majority of the strongest desires from which men act.

This objection, however, loses most of its force as soon as it is realized that the satisfaction of a desire is not its object, and that it is not, in any case, a feeling, nor any other kind of mental state. The satisfaction of a desire, which is its annihilation, is the mere result of its attaining its object, which is the existence of a state of affairs which does not yet exist. This state of affairs may be a mental state of the agent, but it need not be so, and very often is not. Moreover, in the case of coercion, the man who coerces is not usually interested in the state of mind of his victim, but merely wishes him to produce a change in the external world, and the victim, by compliance, usually wishes to prevent the other from acting in such a way as to cause him pain, that is to say, on Broad's view, from causing to arise in his mind feelings which he desires should not exist in it. So that on this view a very large number of unfree actions are necessarily painful, for they must, at the very least, include all actions which are not free on the narrower secondary definition of freedom given in the last chapter, since all these involve fear.

Broad's distinction would, in fact, only allow us to say that unfree actions are pleasanter than free ones under certain clearly defined circumstances, which are not likely to occur very often. If a primary desire which takes effect in unfree action should have as its object the existence of a certain emotion in the mind of the subject of the desire, that emotion will, when it comes into existence, be pleasant by definition, and the degree of its pleasantness will vary directly with the strength of the desire. Thus this unfree action will be pleasanter and, therefore, since pleasure alone is being taken into account, better than a possible alternative free action only if the victorious primary desire is stronger than the secondary desire, whose object is its annihilation, together with the secondary desire of the free action in question. If the object of the strongest primary desire of the free action should itself be an emotion or feeling, the unfree action would be better than it only if its victorious primary desire were stronger than its own secondary desire plus the primary and secondary desires of the free action; so that, since most primary desires have not emotions or feelings for their objects, it is clear that free actions are, on this view, likely to be pleasanter than unfree ones, which are, in fact, very often painful. Hence, other things being equal, it is every man's duty to behave in such a way as to enable other men to act from desired and neutral motives rather than from undesired ones.

But it is not clear that, even if Broad's account of pleasure and pain be true, we are entitled to use it in this way to establish that free actions are, as such, much more likely to be pleasant than unfree ones. For it may be that desires are not to be numbered amongst the mental states which are pleasant or unpleasant according as to whether their continued existence or their annihilation is desired. It is possible that only emotions and feelings, which can be objects of desire, but never themselves desires, can be pleasant and unpleasant. For it is significant that we do not often speak of pleasant and painful desires, and that, when we do so, we generally believe that we are using elliptical phrases, so as not to have to speak of desires accompanied by pleasant or painful emotions. Desire is not often referred to as a species of emotion or feeling, and the ordinary use of language must incline us to the view that men do not normally believe anything to be pleasant or painful except an emotion or a feeling.[1] Things other than emotions and feelings which are called pleasant or painful receive these names because they are believed to be causally related to them.

Moreover, it may be argued that the object of a secondary desire is not necessarily the continued existence or annihilation of a primary desire. A man may desire that a certain other desire should not take effect in action, without necessarily desiring its annihilation. This, of course, is not impossible, but the objection is not very important. For, in the first place, in the case of free actions a man cannot desire that a certain other desire should take effect in action without also desiring its continued existence which is a necessary means to its doing so. So that half the objection is invalid. On the other hand, though it is not impossible that a man should desire that one of his desires should not take effect in action and yet not desire its annihilation, it is extremely unlikely that he would say to himself that it is only necessary for it to be weakened without being destroyed, or for other desires to be strengthened, to ensure its not taking effect in action. Kant would, of course, in the interests of virtue, have preferred evil desires to remain strong and to be conquered by stronger good ones. But, then, few men are philosophers, and few philosophers are heroic.

The final and sufficient objection to using Broad's definitions of pleasure and pain for establishing the superiority of free over unfree actions is that they are probably false. For,

---

[1] A feeling is supposed to be located in some part of the percipient's body. An emotion is not supposed to be located anywhere, though it is often accompanied by feelings. But ordinary language does not always adhere to this distinction. An emotion is often called a feeling, though a localized feeling is never called an emotion.

since the object of a desire does not exist in the time during which it is desired, it is difficult to understand how its being desired can make it pleasant. Yet the emotions and feelings called pleasant are supposed to be pleasant while they exist, so that Broad is committed to saying that their pleasantness consists not in their being desired, but in their having been desired.[1] This is not logically impossible, but it is very probably false.

Nor can the difficulty be set aside by the contention that it is the continuance of an emotion which is desired, for, since an emotion is not merely the object of a mental event but is itself one, it must be made up of numerically different phases, so that to desire its continuance is not to desire the continued existence of a datum which already exists but the continuance of an homogeneous process which has already begun. But this, of course, is merely to desire the future existence of something qualitatively, but not numerically, identical with what already exists.

But even if the object of our awareness, whilst we are conscious of a feeling, were numerically identical at different times, to desire its continuance would not be to desire anything which already exists, for what we should be desiring would be to be conscious of that feeling in the future, and this consciousness does not exist while we desire it.

Moreover, there is the further difficulty that a painful feeling may be one that we have desired to experience. For if we suppose that our experiencing it will help us to realize some end we very strongly desire to realize, we may wish to experience this painful feeling as a means to this end. The fact that we desired it as a means, and not for its own sake, makes no difference at all, for, whatever our ultimate reason for desiring it, the fact remains that we do desire it. So that, if a feeling is pleasant because we desire it, it must be so

[1] He might, however, maintain that a feeling is pleasant not because it has been desired but because similar feelings are desired in the future. This view would be still less plausible.

whatever the cause of the desire. There may also exist in our minds a desire to avoid experiencing this painful feeling, but it must be weaker than our desire to experience it if, in fact, the latter happens to be victorious.

And, lastly, it must not be forgotten that the evidence of everyday language is against Broad, for most persons believe that they often desire things because they are pleasant, and never believe that they are pleasant because they desire them. A man will go for a country walk and will call it pleasant because the walk will excite in him emotions and feelings which please him, but he will not believe that they please him because he wished to experience them.

But even if we can make no use of Broad's definitions,[1] it is still possible that free actions are, on the whole, better than unfree ones, because they are, all things considered, more likely to be pleasant and less likely to be painful. For it may be that action from a desired motive is nearly always accompanied by an emotion which is always pleasant, and that action from an undesired motive is always accompanied by one which is always painful when it accompanies it, but is not necessarily so under other circumstances.[2] Action from a neutral motive may be accompanied by no such emotion at all, and, on this supposition, would, as such, be neither pleasant nor painful, but merely indifferent.

It seems highly probable that actions from desired motives are nearly always accompanied by such an emotion, and those from undesired motives by such another. This latter is usually called 'a feeling of frustration', but it is more difficult to find a convenient name for the former, since none appears to be in everyday use. Perhaps, all things considered, it will be found least inconvenient to call it a feeling of spontaneity, provided that it is understood to be an emotion and nothing more.

[1] Definitions which he intended should meet real difficulties, which we have not attempted to meet. And it should be observed that, if true, they would meet them, though, unfortunately, they happen to be false.
[2] The necessity for making these qualifications will appear later.

We have not defined freedom and the lack of it in terms of those emotions, because many free actions (i.e. all those from neutral motives) are not accompanied by a feeling of spontaneity, and also because ordinary language seems to regard one of these emotions as the effect of unfree actions. For it is quite commonly said that a man feels frustrated because he is unfree,[1] so that a distinction is made between the lack of freedom and the emotion which accompanies it. The connexion between freedom and the feeling of spontaneity is one to which ordinary language hardly ever makes reference, for the reason that it is only some free actions which are accompanied by it. Introspection should convince any one that such an emotion does exist, though it is likely that he will be much less easily convinced that it is the usual accompaniment of actions from desired motives. This is a point which does not seem fully clear, but it is not of extreme importance. It may be true that the emotion sometimes accompanies actions from neutral motives, and quite often does not accompany those from desired motives. But it is clear that it never accompanies unfree actions, though it must always accompany some action or other, so that it follows that freedom is a necessary, though not, perhaps, sufficient, cause of its existence. No more than this need be conceded, and it is enough for our purpose.

Now it is likely that these emotions are good and evil, not only because they are pleasant and unpleasant, but also in respect of their own intrinsic qualities. For men approve of freedom and disapprove of coercion altogether out of proportion to the pleasure and pain which they involve. Coercion is supposed to be a greater evil than toothache, though the pain involved may be no greater. So also this feeling of spontaneity is considered a great good even when it does not cause much pleasure.

[1] This, however, is not strictly true. Though this emotion always accompanies unfree actions, and, when it does so, is always painful, it also sometimes accompanies free actions and is pleasant.

The fact that ordinary people value anything out of proportion to its pleasantness does not prove that it is good apart from the pleasure which it provides,[1] for it is not unusual for people to consider good what in fact is evil or indifferent. But it is at least evidence in favour of the contention that it is good if it is allowed that most of the things which men call good are good, and that few of the things to which they refuse that title actually deserve it. They may sometimes be mistaken when they assert that a particular thing is an instance of a kind of thing which they call good, but they are seldom mistaken in their universal judgements of value when they assert that all things of a certain kind are good. For, after all, unless erroneous judgements were less frequent than correct ones, it would be impossible for persons to communicate with each other, since the only way in which we learn what a word means is by hearing it used in reference to a particular kind of thing in the great majority of cases when it is used.[2]

The main strength of the plea of those philosophers who say that they must always bear the ordinary use of language in mind, not merely as the starting-point of their inquiry, but also as a rough criterion of its success, rests upon this fact, which no man ought to deny, that men do, on the whole, mean the same things by the same words and that their statements are less often false than true. For, if this were not so, philosophers could never have begun to philosophize, for the plain reason that these statements must be the material of their inquiry, for it is in their further analysis that philosophy consists. This, however, does not mean that popular definitions are likely to be correct, but merely that all definitions of ordinary words must necessarily be analyses of popular meanings. For this is the real claim of common sense upon the philosopher. If he appears to be in

[1] Unless, of course, good is taken to mean 'approved of' or 'valued'.

[2] For instance, if most of the things which a man calls 'sticky' do not possess the property which he means by that word, it is impossible for any one else to know what he means by it.

conflict with it, the burden of the proof rests with him. But the claim, though strong, must not be exaggerated. At the present moment we are making no more than a very moderate use of it, for we are saying, in effect, that there is reason to believe that all unfree actions and many free ones involve more evil and more good than can be accounted for by the pain and pleasure which result from them, because men actually put a disvalue and a value upon them out of proportion to these latter.

We have argued that all unfree actions are a means to evil and that some free actions are a means to good, but we have not considered the possibility that they might also be good in themselves. It may be that action from undesired desire is itself evil, and action from desired desire itself good, quite apart from the evil and good of the emotions which are their constant or very usual accompaniments. And it may be that these emotions are evil and good only to the extent to which they are painful and pleasant, and that the excess disvaluation and valuation placed upon these kinds of actions is so placed, not on account of any further evil or goodness in the accompanying emotions, but on their own account. The fact that this excess valuation is put upon them is evidence, so far as it goes, that they involve more evil than pain and more good than pleasure, but it cannot provide us with a clue to whether this excess evil and good qualify the accompanying emotions or the actions themselves. It is likely that they qualify the emotions, for it is doubtful whether the mere fact of its motive[1] being specially related to another desire can make an action either evil or good.

The contention that the emotion of spontaneity need not always, though it very usually does, accompany actions from desired motives is borne out by what are usually called masochistic experiences. Some men, and an even larger number of women, sometimes desire to act from a motive which consists in the desire to avoid certain threatened and

[1] Used here in the sense of a desire to which effect is given in action.

painful consequences. Now this motive from which most men do not usually desire to act is always accompanied by the emotion of frustration even in those cases when men do wish to act from it. But, in these cases, it ceases to be painful and becomes pleasant, and can, in fact, afford very intense pleasure to a certain type of person. So that we have free actions (from desired motives) accompanied by a pleasant emotion which, when it accompanies unfree actions which it always does, is necessarily painful.

Now this emotion of frustration which is pleasant when it accompanies masochistic experiences is still thought to be evil by most people, so that the evil in it cannot possibly be pain. This, therefore, is fairly strong evidence in favour of the view that the two emotions specially connected with free and unfree actions are good and evil in excess of the pleasure and pain involved in them. It seems probable that they are so, sometimes so very greatly in excess of the pleasure and pain involved that these latter form only a very small part of the goodness or evil in question.

Our conclusion, then, is that free actions are, on the whole, preferable to unfree ones on the ground that the latter always involve some evil, whereas the former sometimes involve some good and hardly ever, in respect of their very freedom, involve any evil. This may not seem a sufficiently pleasant conclusion to those who have acquired the capacity to react very strongly to such words as freedom and slavery when they are used on appropriate emotional occasions, but it constitutes a very much stronger argument in favour of freedom than might at first sight appear. For, if it is once allowed that these emotions are amongst the very best and the very worst which it is possible to experience (and all the evidence goes to show that they have been thought to be so by most men), then there is always a very strong case for not depriving a man of his freedom, since the evil involved by its loss can only be offset by a very considerable amount of good.

CHAPTER VII
POLITICAL OBLIGATION

OUR purpose in this chapter will be to find out to what extent the fact that the governors are chosen by the governed to rule over them increases the latter's obligation to obey them. We will, however, take into account only those special goods directly promoted by the fact that the governors have been chosen by their subjects; for the general question as to whether, apart from these goods, representative governments are better than oligarchic or autocratic ones must be answered by historians, if, indeed, there is sufficient evidence to enable them to do so. We will, however, in an appendix to this chapter suggest that this question is very difficult to answer and that, therefore, since certain special goods are promoted by the existence of government by consent, it has an initial advantage over all other forms.

Let us begin by an attempt to elucidate just how the duty to promote one particular good, which accompanies many free actions, and to avoid one particular evil, which accompanies all unfree ones, affects the connexion between consent and political obligation.

It is a commonplace that all government involves coercion and that the individual is constantly performing actions which cannot be included in the class of free actions as it has here been described. The government is continually creating conditions which either prevent their subjects from doing what they want to do, or else cause them to act from motives from which they do not desire to act, so that they come to believe that they are acting 'against their wills'. This belief, for all its absurdity, is none the less a sure sign that its holder is not acting freely, which fact, as we have attempted to show, involves a special evil. But since the government is nothing more than a body of men co-operating for the realization of certain ends, it is obvious that its duty to promote good and avoid evil is precisely similar to that of all other men. It is, therefore, in duty bound not to coerce others, except in cases where the good to be obtained through coercion cannot be obtained in any other way and is greater than the evil which is involved in the actual coercion.

The right of each individual to act freely must be reconciled, so far as it can be, with the necessity of organization and co-operation in the interests of all. There are many ends the realization of which involves the organization and co-operation of many men, and which they ought to pursue because their realization would be good. But all organization involves coercion, because co-operation is possible only if those who co-operate conform to certain rules. When their desire to pursue other incompatible ends inclines them to disobey these rules, they must be supplied with motives for desisting from doing so. Unfortunately human nature is such that conformity to common rules can often be obtained only by causing to arise, in the minds of the recalcitrant, motives for performing the actions which will promote the ends in view, which consist in desires to avoid certain threatened painful consequences of non-performance. It is a psychological and historical fact that it is often impossible to cause others to conform to rules which must be maintained with the object of attaining the greatest good of the greatest number, excepting through coercion of them.

But if some coercion is always necessary, the duty to abstain from it, so far as possible, still remains. Co-operation should be undertaken under such conditions that the greatest possible number of the actions which it involves are the effects of desired and neutral motives. If the ends for the attainment of which the co-operation exists are to be realized under such conditions as will ensure that the least possible amount of coercion will take place, it will be necessary, so far as may be, to obtain the consent of those who co-operate to the enforcement of the rules to which they are to conform. To the extent to which such consent can be obtained, conformity to the rules is achieved without coercion, because the motives from which the consenting parties conform will be such that they desire to act from them or, at least, do not desire not to do so. That is to say, they are, in conforming to the rules, acting freely, so that, to the other goods to which their actions are a means, must be added that good which is the usual accompaniment of actions from desired motives. And, of course, no evil resulting from the lack of freedom need be deducted from them.

Those who enforce conformity to the rules have a general duty to promote the good. Within this more general duty is included the less general one of acting in such a way as to coerce others to the least possible extent. But they often cannot act at all unless they are prepared to act upon their fellow men, and sometimes to act upon them in such a way as to interfere with their freedom. They can, therefore, reconcile their duty to promote other goods with their duty to promote freedom only to the extent to which they act according to the expressed wishes of their fellows. Whenever they act in this way their right to do so depends not only upon their duty to promote goods other than freedom, but also upon their duty to promote freedom; for they can justify their actions by enumerating not only the other goods to which they are a means, but also the evils of coercion which they have avoided. Thus we have here one reason why this expression of their wishes by their fellows ceases to be a mere expression of their wishes and becomes consent, since it increases the governors' right to govern.

To put the argument in another way. Every man has a right to act freely. He has, therefore, there being no other relevant considerations, a right against his fellows that they should not act in such ways as will interfere with his freedom. From this it follows that he has a right against them that they should, as far as possible, obtain his approval of their actions to the extent to which they affect him. This approval, by increasing or creating in them the right to act in these particular ways, constitutes consent. But this consent will not always suffice to give them the right to act in these ways, although its grant to them will necessarily strengthen any right to do so which they may already possess. For if one man has a right against all other men that they should not interfere with his freedom, he has a right against them that they should, so far as they can, obtain his consent to actions on their part which might otherwise injure him in this right. If they act with his consent, they cannot injure him in this right, for then they can claim that he is equally responsible for their actions with themselves.

At this stage it may be objected that an autocrat, provided he always makes those laws which the majority of his subjects desire him to make, will promote the special good which often accompanies free actions and will avoid the special evil which always accompanies unfree ones, just as effectively as any representative government. His doing what his subjects wish him to do, by promoting this good and avoiding this evil, will, on our definition of rights, increase his right to govern them and, therefore, their duty to obey him.

This objection has much to recommend it. An autocrat is able to do a great deal to promote freedom and avoid coercion, though his giving effect to his subjects' expressed wishes (they would have to be expressed for him to know what they were) could not be said to constitute consent. But it still remains true that consent is the best guarantee of freedom, and that, other things being equal, no autocrat, so long as he remains an autocrat, can possibly safeguard freedom as efficiently as a representative government.

The reason for this disadvantage on the part of the autocrat is psychological. If a man believes that the ruler who is giving effect to his wishes could just as easily do the opposite, then the ruler is less able to create the conditions which most efficiently safeguard the subject's freedom. If he imposes laws on his subjects which they would impose upon themselves, it does not follow that they obey his laws from the same motives as they would obey their own. It is a psychological fact, whose existence will not be denied by any one who troubles to introspect, that men reconcile themselves more easily to obeying persons whose power to give orders is dependent upon their wishes that they should do so than to obeying those who they think could still compel them to obey even if they did not happen to be giving effect to their wishes. To convince oneself of this fact it is only necessary to order some one upon pain of punishment to do what he already intended to do. Of course, representative governments also give orders upon pain of punishment, but those who elected them intended that they should do so.

Moreover, even when a representative government is coercing a man who voted for it, the very knowledge that it is acting with his consent makes the coercion more easily tolerable than it would otherwise have been. For he knows that he was partly responsible for its being in the position to coerce him, and that he is, therefore, indirectly responsible for its present action, and this knowledge is such as to make the coercion less painful. This is a psychological fact of the first importance, especially in the case of reflective persons who feel themselves less frustrated by those who are doing what they themselves wished them to be able and empowered them to do, and which there is some likelihood of their being prevented from doing in the future. The man who has a sense of justice, and most men have it to some degree, is inclined to submit himself more easily to the consequences of his own action, which are not, after all, unforeseen. It may have been some consideration of this sort which led Rousseau to assert that, in a democracy, the citizen, when he was being compelled to obey the law, was being 'forced to be free'. The phrase is self-contradictory. Molière put the point better when he wrote 'Tu l'as voulu, George Dandin', for it never occurred to him to write, 'Tu le veux'.

Of course, in the case of the benevolent autocrat, if he made it his principle of action to do always what the majority of his subjects desired, if he took trouble to set up some sort of machinery to discover what they did in fact wish him to do, and if they were convinced that this was his principle of action from which he would never depart, then the autocrat would be acting with this majority's consent, because the conditions under which he acted would ensure their being indirectly responsible for his actions. But in so far as he did so he would cease to be an autocrat and would become the mere agent of his people. He would be in the same position as the King of England, in whose name all laws are made, but who has practically nothing to do with the making of any of them. But an autocrat is a ruler who is able to make a law even when the great majority of his subjects are opposed to it. He is such that, when he does make a law that they wish him to make, his doing so is still a very imperfect safeguard of their freedom. For it is not as likely that a man will obey a law from a motive from which he desires to obey it, when he is obeying an autocrat, as when he is obeying men whom he chose to be legislators. Now it is apparent that the despot, being a despot, however benevolent he may be, does not, when he is giving effect to the wishes of a majority of his subjects, act in such a way as to cause them to believe that they are the real authors of the law.

Besides, even if a man obeys a despot from a desired motive, it does not follow that his doing so would, there being no other relevant considerations, promote as great a good as if he were obeying governors whom he helped to choose. For the emotion of spontaneity is not always of equal strength, whatever the action from a desired motive which it accompanies. It is sometimes very intense, and at other times very weak, and it is again a psychological fact that it is, on the whole, more intense when it accompanies acts of obedience to laws for the existence of which a man can regard himself as partly responsible than when it accompanies acts of obedience to those laws which were made without his consent. Nor does religious experience weaken this argument. What are called the laws of God, or, at least, those of them which are not enforced by the government, are obeyed only by persons who freely accept them as principles which ought to govern their actions, except to the extent to which the fear of hell causes them to be obeyed. But the fear of post-mortem punishment has always, even in the days when religious beliefs were most intense, been less efficacious as an inducement to obey God's laws than either the belief of religious persons that they ought to be obeyed or the fear of earthly punishment.

There is also a great deal to be said for the contention that it is often less painful to obey laws that are made by the representatives of the majority of the community, even for persons who did not elect these representatives and actually disapprove of their laws. For, in the first place, directly democratic and representative governments are more easily alterable in their composition, so that those who dislike their policies have better reason for hoping that they can cause them to be reversed. No doubt Mme de Pompadour could more easily influence the ruler of France than the modern liberal can influence the present British government, but, on the whole, the ordinary member of the democratic state, since his opinions are usually shared by a considerable number of his fellow subjects, has more reason to hope that their repeated expression will have some effect upon his governors. It may be true that he may, very often, have very small grounds for this hope, but this is quite compatible with his having less grounds under an autocracy or oligarchy. It may even be true that an intelligent man has more chance of influencing an autocrat or a government of oligarchs[1] than of influencing the rulers of a democracy, but this does not affect our argument. We are not concerned with the powers of a small minority, but with those of the large majority of the members of a community which is composed of groups which have at one time or another disliked the enforcement of certain laws, and whose members have had greater reason to hope that their wishes would have some effect upon the actions of present and future governments than they would have had had they not been members of a democratic state. It does not matter to what extent propaganda influences them, for, whatever the origin of their wishes and however little the putting of them into effect would benefit them, yet, since the expression of these wishes must have a considerable effect upon the government, there does exist this hope. And in so far as it exists, it makes more tolerable the restraints which those who suffer them believe may be abolished in the future.

Besides, the very knowledge that whenever many persons co-operate for the furtherance of certain ends most of them must expect that, at some time or other, they will be called upon to perform actions of which they disapprove does, to a certain extent, reconcile them to this performance, and so ensures either that it will be free, or else, if unfree, that the emotion of frustration will be considerably diminished in intensity. Of course, this knowledge may not always influence those who disapprove of the actions in question, but to the extent to which it does so, it either makes their obedience free or else diminishes the evil resulting from the necessary interference with their freedom.

The knowledge on the part of the subject of a benevolent autocrat that obedience to a law of which he disapproves will promote more good than disobedience may ensure that his

---

[1] Though there is very little, if any, evidence to support the view that this is generally the case.

obedience is free, that is to say, that the actions constituting this obedience are performed from desired motives. No one denies this. But in a democracy one of the ends of government is the enforcement of laws which give effect to the wishes of as many of the governed as possible, and a necessary means to this end is the obedience of every citizen even to those laws which do not give effect to his wishes. So that the knowledge that the greatest freedom of the greatest number cannot be achieved except at the occasional expense of the freedom of the few itself diminishes this expense, for it helps to promote those conditions in which even those who disapprove of the laws obey them from desired or neutral motives, or else from undesired motives accompanied by a less intense emotion of frustration than might otherwise be the case. This is again a psychological fact. The statement of it in the terms in which we have defined freedom and the lack of it and the good and evil attendant upon them may appear complicated. But the fact itself is simple, and is attested by almost every one. For it amounts to no more than this, that most persons, other considerations being irrelevant, submit themselves more readily to the wishes of a majority than to those of a minority in circumstances in which they are members of neither.

It is not asserted that government by the consent of the majority of the governed always safeguards freedom better than an oligarchy or autocracy could do under any conceivable circumstances. An autocrat may make very few laws, and those, most of them, such that nearly all his subjects obey them willingly. On the other hand, a representative government may exercise an intolerable tyranny over the unrepresented minority. But a representative government can only tyrannize over a minority, whereas an autocracy or oligarchy can sometimes do so over a large majority of the governed. The contention, then, amounts merely to this, that, other things being equal, government by consent is more likely to safeguard freedom than is any other sort.

For, since laws must be made and since, by their very nature, they must place restrictions upon the freedom of those persons who can be compelled to obey them, it is clear that the best way of diminishing the number of these restrictions is to ensure that they give effect to the wishes of as many of the governed as possible.

The arguments here advanced in favour of government by consent as against all other forms of government apply not merely to this kind of organization, but also to all other kinds. Whenever men co-operate to promote certain ends, rules of action must be enforced upon them as a necessary means to the achievement of these ends. These rules should, whatever the type of organization concerned, be enforced as far as possible with the consent of the majority of the persons who may be called upon to obey them. History shows us that most organizations have imposed and still impose rules to which the majority of their members have not consented. The contention is often advanced that these organizations would never achieve their ends, if those who controlled them were obliged to obtain the consent of the majority of the persons they controlled. There may be some justification for this view, but it is based upon very slight evidence. For the democratization of these organizations has hardly ever been tried, and when it has been, nearly always under special conditions very unlikely to make it a success. Nor has there ever been made a really serious attempt to prepare the conditions of its success by the systematic and intelligent education of the majority of mankind. A certain amount of information has been given to the citizens of industrially advanced communities so that they should become more efficient workmen, but it has seldom occurred to the rich to improve their general intellectual abilities.

It is to be hoped that the main advantage of government by consent has been adequately explained. If freedom is not very well safeguarded in modern democracies, this does not invalidate the arguments which have been advanced. For it must be remembered that only one important form of social organization is ruled with the consent of a majority (and sometimes of only a large minority) of its members. Nor must it be forgotten that this organization, though it is legally supreme, affects the day-to-day life of its members in a less direct and visible manner than some of the others which are very far from being democratic. Far too many of the arguments of persons who nowadays consider themselves too shrewd to be taken in by democracy are not really aimed at the system which they desire to destroy. For what they mostly prove, or, rather, attempt to prove, is that what appears to be democracy is not really so at all. From this they arrive at either of two strange conclusions: that democracy ought to be done away with, or else that something which does not appear to be democracy, but really is so, ought to be set up in its place.

However this may be and whatever the state of the world at present, the fact remains that people do set great store by freedom and that there is only one means of reconciling it with the necessity of co-operation in the interests of all. That this means, if put into effective practice, also ensures that most of the co-operators will have promised obedience to those who govern their common activities is considered by most people an additional advantage. From which it follows that the governors derive their right to govern not only from the fact that they are restraining freedom as little as may be, but also from these same promises. And most people, whatever their belief as to the proper definitions of moral notions, agree that promises ought to be kept.

An abstract discussion of consent and political obligation, such as this, often awakens a certain distaste in the mind of the reader. The glib use of such words as 'right' and 'good', the assumption that they have *absolute* and *objective* meanings, and the erection, upon the foundation of a number of platitudes, of a system of ideas which is certainly not new and which appears trivial and verbose, must annoy all sensitive persons. But it must be remembered that the mere use of these words and phrases does not bind the user to any particular interpretation of them. Whatever the words 'good' and 'right' may mean, whether the reader is an intuitionist, an ideal utilitarian, or a subjectivist convinced that all Professor Moore's arguments against the so-called naturalistic fallacy miss the point, it still remains true that such words are used and have meanings and that the mere use of them does not make nonsense of the sentences which include them. In this book there are only three words of which a definition is offered. They are 'consent', 'freedom', and 'right' (in the sense of the word which is not synonymous with 'morally obligatory').

Constant discussion, much of it pedantic, always awakens in sensitive persons a distaste for the 'key' words and phrases around which it revolves.[1] Much the same causes prepare the decline of a philosophical epoch as of an artistic or literary one. But, unfortunately, men are continually ensnared by words. Philosophers whose chief claim to our gratitude is that they have shown us that many old problems were unreal and merely verbal prepare new problems for us which are just as obscure and for exactly the same reasons. Just as the philosopher must protect himself against the attractions of words and phrases which stimulate his imagination, but to which he can attach no precise meaning, so also he must learn to discount his prejudice against those which have no disadvantage except that they are a little the worse for wear.

The sense of the *unreality* of this discussion may also be diminished if the reader remembers that this book is primarily interested in definitions and abstractions. Whether or not so-called democratic governments do or do not really

[1] Many false theories, however ingenious in themselves, are sufficiently refuted by platitudes. One or two of them, much too familiar by this time, have ruined Hegelianism.

govern with the consent of the majority of their subjects is a practical and irrelevant matter.

It will have been noticed that this chapter contains even more commonplaces than the others. The need for their frequent repetition results from the fact that persons who acknowledge their incompetence in logic and mathematics slake their thirst for the abstract by indulging in political philosophy and by trying, by means of obscure utterances, to make it appear more difficult than it is.

APPENDIX TO CHAPTER VII

BEFORE ending this book it is necessary to consider the statement, so often made by apologists for democracy, that a government which is popularly elected is more likely to govern in the interests of a majority of the governed than is any other kind. This statement was never made by any one more confidently than by Bentham, who advocated universal suffrage, not from any belief in the natural rights of men, but for strictly utilitarian reasons. One of the conditions, and the most important, of obtaining the greatest happiness of the greatest number was, he thought, the establishment of a democratic form of government. Man, he maintained, desires his own happiness, so that, if he has the power to elect his governors, he will see to it that the persons he elects govern in such a way as not to deprive him of it, but rather to give him every opportunity of increasing it. But all other men will do the same, so that, since no man will be able to achieve his own happiness to the detriment of that of other people, the greatest happiness of the greatest number will necessarily be ensured. On the other hand, a government which is the agent of only a small proportion of the nation is likely to sacrifice the happiness of the majority in its efforts to satisfy the minority upon which its power depends.

The peculiar theory of the moral nature of man which he shared with many of his contemporaries and notably with Adam Smith, coupled with his lack of experience of popular government, naturally led Bentham to conclude that democracy, direct or indirect, would necessarily promote the greatest happiness of the greatest number. But the problem cannot be solved by *a priori* arguments, for it is essentially empirical. The question to ask is: 'Are representative governments or direct democracies in fact better means to the desired end than are any possible alternatives?' (The desired end will here be taken to be the greatest good of the greatest number, and not merely the greatest happiness as with Bentham.) An absolutely certain answer to this question cannot possibly be given. Whether or not democracy will promote more good than, for instance, autocracy, will in both cases depend upon the character of the people concerned, and in the second case upon that of the autocrat. Even Mill thought representative government desirable only in countries in which the majority of the people were sufficiently advanced to enable it to function properly. He did not argue that, owing to the peculiar character of man, popular government would necessarily promote the greatest happiness of the greatest number. He thought that it would do so only under certain circumstances.

But, since he was a hedonist, Mill could take into account nothing save pleasure, the only thing which he acknowledged to be good. On the other hand, as soon as it is admitted that there are other goods besides pleasure, it becomes possible to maintain that, other things being equal, popular governments are necessarily better than any other, since they involve less interference with men's freedom. They also involve a greater interest in the general welfare on the part of the governed and an actual participation in the attempts made to promote it, which may be good quite apart from any question of the goodness of their consequences. But it is especially the fact that they tend to avoid the destruction of freedom, which is a great good, which marks their superiority over any other form of government, so long as there are no other considerations to be taken into account. And even when other goods come to be considered, an autocratic or oligarchic form of government must promote them very much more efficiently than would a popular one before its existence and continuance can be shown to be desirable.

Apologists of popular government have usually ignored the particular goods mentioned above, which are directly connected with the fact of consent, and have attempted to prove its superiority over other kinds of government by maintaining that it is the most likely to promote other goods which we have so far not taken into account. Hedonists like Bentham and Mill, as well as political thinkers as different from them as Green and Bosanquet, have favoured government by the consent of the majority on the ground that it is, with certain qualifications, the best means to the goods which they suppose to be the only proper ends of government. The goods they had in mind, though they differed greatly from each other, certainly did not include any which we have attempted to show are directly connected with democracy.[1]

But, leaving these latter goods out of account, it is very doubtful whether popular government is in fact more likely than any other kind to promote the good, even in highly civilized communities. In the first place it is very doubtful whether men really are good judges

---

[1] The terms 'democracy' and 'popular government' are here used in the same meaning.

of their own interests. They may not even recognize the good when they come across it; they may set great store by what is worthless or evil,[1] and, should they be so enlightened as to estimate things at their proper value, they may be quite ignorant of the most efficient means of obtaining the goods which they desire. If they are in a position to choose their own governors, there is no particular reason for supposing that their choice is likely to be a good one. Indeed, since the majority of people everywhere, however excellent the education they may have obtained, are of very restricted intelligence, it is more likely than not that they will not only be ignorant of the best means to the good, but also of the good itself. An educated person, because he thinks about more things, has more opinions than an uneducated one, but there is little reason for supposing that he is more likely to be right about matters that interest them both. He is just as likely to be wrong, but for different and more complicated reasons.

It is often argued that popular governments are more likely than others to remedy their subjects' grievances, but there is as much to be said for the contrary opinion. If a community is industrially and socially advanced, then the majority of its members, whether or not they have the power to elect their rulers, can usually put such pressure upon them that they will make laws in their interest almost as readily as they would were they actually their agents. There is no reason for supposing that Imperial Germany was less well ruled than Republican France, although the governors of the latter country are much more truly the agents of the governed than were those of the former. The desire to placate persons upon whose approval his power, though not his right, to rule depends may lead a ruler to as great an activity on their behalf as if he were their agent. On the other hand, the elected representatives of the people may, either because of their ignorance or because they have deceitfully persuaded the latter to empower them to make laws which benefit only a small class within the community, rule with their subjects' consent in such a way as actually to decrease their good.

Enemies of autocracy have sometimes alleged that a democratic government is the first condition of the flourishing of the arts, which few will deny is a great good. This contention is quite untrue and its falseness is made evident by the most superficial inquiry into the facts. It is far from absurd to suppose that the best literature of the second half of the nineteenth century was produced in Russia,

[1] Provided, of course, that good does not mean 'approved of'

whose autocratic government was held in contempt by every friend of democracy in western Europe. Indeed, most of the great artists, composers, scientists, and men of letters who have created the common stock of European culture lived under governments which were far from representative of the majority of their subjects. Of course, some non-popular governments have actually ruled in such a way as to maintain conditions unfavourable to the development of the arts. But many have done precisely the opposite and have encouraged, or at least have refrained from discouraging, the arts and sciences. Until quite recent times it seldom occurred to autocrats or to governing cliques and classes that architecture, painting, or music could be seditious, and they mostly confined themselves to placing severe restrictions upon the freedom of philosophers, theologians, politicians, and social thinkers. To the extent to which religious bodies were hostile to the unrestricted activities of artists, writers, and scientists, they seem to have been so in democratic countries quite as much as in monarchies and oligarchies. On the whole, it appears that both non-popular and popular governments have often been hostile to the development of certain of the sciences, but that they have seldom hindered the progress of the arts provided that they have not been of an obviously propagandist nature. On the other hand, in so far as the actual encouragement of the arts is concerned, oligarchies have a better record than democracies and for an obvious reason. Hitherto only a small section of the community has possessed leisure and so been enabled to acquire an understanding of the productions of artists, philosophers, and writers of the sort which is, and not merely financially, an important condition of their being able to do justice to their talents. The achievements of the Athenian oligarchy[1] during the fifth century B.C. constitute one of the strongest arguments in favour of the contention that popular government is not a necessary condition of the flourishing of the arts.

It would be unwise of persons wishing to bring forward evidence in support of the contention that non-popular government is dangerous to culture to refer to the activities of the present rulers of Germany. Hitler and his accomplices achieved power because they were supported by a larger proportion of the German people than was any other party.[2] They were members of the Reichstag at the time

---

[1] Usually called a democracy, because the existence of a large majority of slaves and women is conveniently forgotten.

[2] The stupid attitude of the present rulers of Germany to modern art and literature is largely due to the accident that, of the three most important of

when they took over the government of Germany, and so were just as truly the agents of the persons who elected them as are the members of the government coalition in the House of Commons. And, even if they did not then represent an absolute majority of the electorate, the parliamentary supporters of several British governments have been in exactly the same case.

The friends of democracy sometimes criticize autocratic governments on the ground that they are more likely than popular ones to degenerate, since a great ruler or king is as likely as not to be succeeded by a very mediocre person. This, of course, is true, but it is no less true that the agents of the majority of the governed are not likely to be very superior to their electors, either morally or intellectually. Indeed, though they are usually not below the average as far as their intelligence goes, they are often persons of very low character. Moreover, it must be remembered that autocrats also rule through a multitude of agents, who may sometimes include among them men of exceptional ability, who, if they are able to secure their master's confidence, may rule absolutely to the great benefit of the governed. It also quite often happens that monarchs and autocrats are much more open to certain kinds of new ideas than are large assemblies, for the reason that it is easier to persuade one man than six hundred. The French monarchs maintained the finest system of roads in Europe, they rebuilt large sections of Paris.[1] The Prussian kings abolished feudalism, they built up a very efficient system of education and the most competent of European civil services.

In England democracy was no better thought of than on the Continent, but the governing oligarchy provided a constant supply of able rulers, who, for all their faults, managed to maintain the peaceful and orderly government which was the first condition of the growth of commerce and industry. In so far as life was easier and more prosperous in this country than on the Continent, this was so, not because the English ruled themselves through agents, but because their social organization was different and because they were

them, one was an unsuccessful painter and another an unsuccessful poet and playwright.

[1] Louis XIV encouraged and supported two of the greatest modern playwrights, of whom one was the greatest of all writers of comedy. Neither the great painters of seventeenth- and eighteenth-century France, who lived under an absolute monarch, nor those of the third republic seem to have been at all interested in, or affected by, the forms of their governments.

free from invasions and from many of the wars upon which the European monarchs, no less than the democratic governments which succeeded them, were constantly engaged.

It would be quite outside the scope of this appendix to undertake a long and careful investigation of history with a view to deciding whether democracies have been more productive of goods besides freedom than have other kinds of government. The very superficial discussion of the last few paragraphs is intended to illustrate the empirical nature of the problem and to suggest that no cursory survey of the functioning of past and present governments will provide us with a solution. At a first glance the available evidence does not appear to favour popular any more than non-popular governments.

There is, therefore, if only the goods usually considered are taken into account, little reason for supposing that, as a general rule, one form of government is better than another. But as soon as we consider not only these goods, but also those which have been shown to be especially connected with government by consent, then the scales are, *ceteris paribus*, weighted in favour of the democratic form. Thus it is that it becomes possible to maintain that, on the whole, a government which is representative of a majority or at least of a large proportion of its subjects has a better claim to the obedience of all than has a government which is representative of none or only of a small number of them.

Moreover, such a government has not only a greater claim to the obedience of those of its subjects whose representative it is, but also to that of all the others, for they too are in duty bound to promote these special goods, even if they do not themselves enjoy them. The obligation of those whose agents the governors are is greater than that of the others, not because the duty to promote one's own good is greater than that to promote other people's, but because they alone can perform their own contracts. That is to say, the special obligation to obey their governors, which is a case of the duty to keep promises, is obviously one which the consenting parties alone can fulfil.

POSTSCRIPT TO THE SECOND EDITION

I

POLITICAL obligation, even in Oxford, is now an old-fashioned topic. T. H. Green lectured on it in the nineteenth century, and some thirty and more years ago H. A. Prichard subjected his lectures to elaborate and severe criticism. This little book, now being printed in a paperback edition, was virtually finished some two years before it was published in 1938. It was considerably influenced by the method, and to some extent even the style, of Professor Prichard. In the chapter on Rights I find myself speaking of ideas that Ritchie is 'failing to express' in his book *Natural Rights*. These words remind me how often Prichard in the lectures I listened to accused Green of 'failing to express' his meaning, and then went on to speak for him just a little and much more against him. This book is much less formidable, much less penetrating, as a criticism of other men's arguments than the powerful attacks launched by Prichard, but it is an attempt to do what he and other philosophers of his time often did supremely well. It is an attempt to elucidate a small number of important ideas by a close examination of how they are used in several well-known theories.

It is much more that than anything else claimed for it when it was first published. Whatever its defects as it goes about the business of analysing such terms as *consent*, *freedom*, and *rights*, its attempts to define them and to distinguish some of their uses in political argument are more perceptive and instructive than anything it has to say about the duty to obey governments that have the consent of their subjects. As an essay on political obligation in representative democracies it leaves too much that is important out of account, and such merits as it may have belong to it mostly as an essay in conceptual analysis.

The book is often unfair, at times to the point of absurdity. Rousseau's doctrine of the general will is much richer in content, much more original and suggestive, than the comments on it in the second chapter give any idea of, and so too is Hegel's theory of the State and what the individual owes to it. To treat such a doctrine or such a theory as an attempt to overcome difficulties which proved too much for Locke is to miss altogether what is really profound and challenging in it. Locke's political philosophy is above all else a theory of political obligation; but Rousseau's is so much less, and Hegel's even less than Rousseau's. The sociologist, the social psychologist, and the historian of ideas are all better equipped to discern what is valuable in the political and social theories of a Rousseau or a Hegel than is the mere student of philosophy with a taste for looking closely at how words are used.

Yet criticism is not always useful in proportion as it is fair. Rousseau who moved into difficult regions into which Locke never ventured also followed in his footsteps, and even Hegel was tempted from time to time to speak darkly about the duty of obedience to governments and to the laws. To treat Rousseau's doctrine of the general will as if it were primarily an attempt to derive the duty of obedience from the fact of consent is to fall far short of the whole truth about it. Yet, though the doctrine does much more than merely attempt to do this, it does also attempt it. It attempts and it fails, and the reasons for this failure need not escape the notice of the critic who takes too narrow a view of the doctrine. So, too, though Hegel, in his *Philosophy of Right*, does much more besides, he also puts forward, obliquely and disingenuously, a theory of political obligation. He does what his two great masters, Plato and Aristotle, never felt the need to do, and he does it because he cannot altogether set aside the question which to political theorists for nearly two hundred years before his time had seemed the most important of all: Why and to what

extent ought men to obey their rulers and the law? Hegel's
equivocal answer to this question is to imply, clearly enough,
that in the fully rational or fully developed State, the citizen
really wills what the law requires of him and is therefore free
when he obeys the law, and then to leave it unclear what the
citizen should do when the State is not fully rational. He is
concerned, as Plato and Aristotle were not, with the problem of how freedom can be reconciled with authority, and
is therefore evasive as they had no need to be. He seeks to
resolve the problem by showing what conditions must hold
if the citizen is to be free, and concludes that he cannot be
free except in a moral and political order which is the
culmination of a necessary process of development. In
reaching this conclusion, he elaborates a conception of
freedom far removed from Locke's idea of it, a conception
open to serious criticism and yet revealing a deeper understanding of what is involved in man's being a social and
moral creature than is to be found in the writings of Locke
and his contemporaries. Nevertheless, this conception, as
Hegel expounds it, has illiberal implications, though he
fails to draw them clearly.

The English Idealists, for obvious reasons, were much
more concerned than Hegel was to show that their con-
ceptions of the State and of freedom were entirely in keep-
ing with the doctrines of government by consent of the
governed and liberty of conscience, doctrines whose greatest
champion had been John Locke. They could not evade, as
Hegel did more or less, the problem which to Locke was
the central problem of political philosophy. They really
faced and tried to answer the question, Why and to what
extent ought men to obey their rulers and the laws? Bosanquet speaks, as Hegel never did, of a *paradox* of self-
government; he is aware of the English audience to whom
he is offering un-English ideas about the State in its relations to the individual. Green speaks at times of self-
perfection in much the same way as John Stuart Mill did,

and he is, for all his Idealism, quite free of idolatry of the State. My book does much less than justice to Bosanquet and to Green. Yet most of their arguments chosen for attack are open to the criticisms made of them, and several are inspired by the wish to show that there is consent or freedom where in fact there is not. Criticism can be unfair in creating an impression that a theory is poorer and cruder than in fact it is, and yet not be misdirected because the confusions and mistakes it points at really do form part of the theory.

In this postscript I shall attempt only two things: to argue that the analysis of political consent offered in this book is in important respects defective, and to indicate briefly some of the reasons for holding that representative democracy, or government with the consent of the governed, is better than any alternative to it, given the conditions of industrial society and the aspirations that men acquire inside it. This book is also, in its narrow way, an argument for representative democracy; but this, as I said earlier, is the more superficial part of it. It would need a long book to make an adequate case for representative government, but a few paragraphs may suffice to suggest how such a case might be made. The account of freedom given in this book is even more defective than the account of consent. But freedom has been much more widely and more perceptively discussed by both philosophers and political theorists than has consent. It is well worth discussing again but only at greater length than the space available to me allows. It is the less neglected and the more difficult topic of the two, and the hope of being able to say something useful about it in a few words is considerably smaller.

Freedom, as it concerns the student of politics, is a matter of rights and opportunities, often difficult to define. In order to define them, he need not take a stand with either determinists or indeterminists in the long controversy between them. Nor has he anything to gain by speaking, as I did in the chapter on Freedom in this book, of desired, undesired, and neutral motives. To define the rights and opportunities which constitute freedom in the senses relevant to his study, he must, of course, define the situations in which men act when they are said to act freely. He must describe accurately both states of mind and social and moral relations. He cannot make do with any such apparently simple definition of freedom as the power to act without constraint by others, nor must he be satisfied with a mere enumeration of rights. He must, for example, make up his mind what conditions must hold if elections are to be accounted *free*; he must look closely at what people say about freedom of thought and expression, about the free choice of a career, and even about self-realization, if he is to define the rights and opportunities they have in mind when they aspire to freedom. He must make some fine distinctions and analyse some of the most often used and important and elusive ideas. His task is formidable and long. He can accomplish it without trailing painfully behind the philosophers in all their controversies, but he must take much more into account than I took when I discussed freedom some thirty years ago.

II

Political consent must be distinguished from mere approval or acquiescence if it is to be possible to distinguish government by consent from other types of government. But I now think it a mistake to speak of it as necessarily the granting of a permission or as involving the expression of a wish. To give permission is to consent but to consent is not always to give permission, though it is always to do or to take part in doing something which the doer knows, or is presumed to know, creates in another a right he would not otherwise have. That is to say, consent is always this in the sense of it which is relevant here, the sense that makes representative government and government by consent synonymous terms.

When a man votes for a successful candidate to an office, he need not express any wish about him; he need do no more than make a mark on a piece of paper or put a pebble into an urn or raise his hand. It might perhaps be said of any one of these actions, that it is an expression of a wish, though not in so many words. Surely, to put a cross against the name *Smith* on a ballot paper at an election is to express the wish that Smith should hold the office for which he is a candidate? But the voter may not want Smith to hold the office; he may think that Smith has no chance of getting elected and may vote for him only for the sake of preventing the election of Brown. Yet, if Smith were in fact elected, it would be odd to say of anyone who had voted for him that he did not consent to his holding the office.

It is true that a man may express a wish in so many words and yet be insincere. He may say to a guest, 'I do wish you would stay', when in fact he wishes him to be gone. There is no denying that he expresses a wish and therefore consents to his guest's staying, however keen he may be to get rid of him. But then, in this case, there is no denying that a wish has been expressed precisely because certain words have been uttered. The consent consists, not in the desire that the guest should stay on, but in the deliberate utterance of these words by someone who knows their meaning. When we say that he expresses a wish, we do not mean that he makes a true statement about his desires; we mean only that he makes a certain kind of statement knowing what it means and under such conditions that he is responsible for certain of its consequences. The making of this statement under these conditions is the expression of a wish. But when a voter puts a cross against a name, he makes no such statement, though he does do something which has or may have certain consequences, and he does it deliberately, knowing that it may have them.

What he does *signifies* something by virtue of rules and procedures which ensure that it has, or may have, this kind of consequence—in this case, the possession of a right by someone who otherwise would not have it; and he knows, or is presumed to know, what it signifies. He deliberately makes a symbolic gesture. If the gesture is to be an act of political consent, it must be a certain kind of gesture. But it need not be the kind which is the expression of a wish.

We often grant a permission by expressing a wish but as often we do not. To say 'you may do this' to someone who otherwise would not have the right to do it, is neither to wish that he should do it nor to express the wish; it is merely to give a permission. It is also, of course, to consent to his doing it. Giving consent is very often granting permission but it is not so always. At least, not unless we stretch the meaning of the words 'to grant permission' to cover cases not usually covered by them. It is unusual, though perhaps allowable, to say of someone who appoints another man to an office that he gives him permission to discharge the duties of that office; it is much more usual to say that he grants authority than that he gives permission. And yet, if he grants authority to another man, he consents to that man's exercise of it. It is odder still, and perhaps not allowable, to say of a voter who, when he casts his vote, is still uncertain which candidate will be elected, that he gives permission to the successful candidate to discharge the duties of his office. Yet he consents to his doing so.

In the first chapter of this book I was so much concerned to argue that Locke and others had given to the word *consent* too wide a sense that I myself gave one that was too narrow. The word is, of course, used in several different senses, and it means nothing to call any of them too wide or too narrow except in relation to some purpose for which it is or might be used. Locke wanted to distinguish rightful government from tyranny, and yet did not wish (as Hobbes had done) to suggest that all government is rightful provided only that it exercises effective power. Yet he gave to the word *consent* so wide a meaning that he could not use it to make the distinction he wanted to make. My purpose was not the same as Locke's. I was not arguing that government, to be rightful, must be with the consent of the governed; I was merely looking for that definition of the word *consent* which makes representative government and government by consent equivalent terms. Moreover, I was not proposing that the word should be used in some new sense over and above the old ones; I was trying to define what I believed to be an ordinary sense of it.

My definition was too narrow. It compelled me to hold, for example, that a man voting for an unsuccessful candidate at an election did not consent to the authority of the elected candidate. If consenting to a man's authority involves expressing the wish that he should exercise it or granting him permission to do so, then clearly the citizen voting for a candidate who is not elected does not consent to the authority of the elected candidate. It would be an abuse of language to suggest the contrary. But if consent does not necessarily involve expressing a wish or granting a permission, then it is no longer clear that the voter for an unsuccessful candidate does not consent to the authority of the successful one. Where there is an established process of election to an office, then, *provided the election is free*, anyone who takes part in the process consents to the authority of whoever is elected to the office. This, I think, is not to ascribe a new meaning to the word *consent* but is only to define a very ordinary and important political use of it. The citizen who votes at an election is presumed to understand the significance of what he is doing, and if the election is free, he has voluntarily taken part in a process which confers authority on someone who otherwise would not have it. He may bitterly regret the election of the successful candidate and may not even have expected it, but if the election was free and he freely took part in it, he consented to the authority of the man elected.

It is a hard task to define the conditions that must hold if an election is to be accounted free, as anyone who has tried to define them will admit. I cannot, in the space available to me, attempt the definition. The point that I now wish to make is merely that one man can quite properly be said to have consented to another man's holding an elected office even though he voted against him at the election. To speak of consent in this way is to make an ordinary use of one of the most important terms in the political vocabulary.

We also quite often, and quite properly, speak of people's consenting to a political system by taking part in its processes, even though they had nothing to do with setting the system up in the first place. This consent, too, is something different from approval. Not all participation, but only participation under certain conditions, constitutes this kind of consent. There is a sense in which everyone who lives in a political community takes part in the political system. If subjects did not obey, governments could not govern. By their obedience subjects sustain the power of their rulers. But they do not therefore consent either to their authority or to the political system which determines the limits of that authority, even though they approve of it. Before they can be said to consent to the political system by taking part in it, there must be legal means available to them of changing the system and of advocating change. If there is nothing they could do without resort to illegality to change the system, then they cannot be said to consent to it, however willing their obedience, however warm their approval.

By consenting to someone's authority, you put yourself under an obligation to do what the possessor of it requires of you, provided the requirement is an exercise of that authority. The obligation to obey does not always, nor even often, derive from consent to authority, but to consent to authority is always to undertake a duty of obedience, even though the duty is not absolute. Yet not all acts which give rise to authority are acts of consent to authority. If we obey someone over a period of time, we make it possible for him to rule us to our benefit, and if he does so rule us, he acquires authority over us and we have a duty of obedience. Yet our obedience is not consent in the sense of the word we are now seeking to define, for it is not the sort of consent that we have in mind when we call representative government, government by consent of the governed. I do not say that we ought not to give the name consent to behaviour which gives rise to authority and to allegiance; I say only that it is consent of a different kind from the kind I tried to analyse in this book. To act in such a way as eventually gives rise to authority and to a duty of obedience is neither to confer authority nor to undertake obedience. It is not the political theorist's business to decide what is to be called consent and what is not, but it is his business to distinguish between the different senses in which the word is used when applied to political behaviour and to point out which sense is relevant in this or that political context.

III

The important question to put about government by consent is not the one put in this book. As this book itself argues, even where government is representative, its subjects consent to the authority of their rulers only to some extent and their duty of obedience arises from other things besides consent. Many governments have not ruled with the consent of their subjects and yet have exercised rightful authority over them. The important question is not, To what extent does the duty of obedience arise from consent? It is much rather, Under what conditions is government by consent more to be desired than other forms of government?

The highly abstract though moderate case for government by consent made in this book is altogether too utilitarian. It relies too much on the argument that, though coercion is painful, it is apt to be less so when those who exercise it get their authority from those over whom they exercise it. No doubt, coercion is painful. But then it is also true that people like to be told what to do provided they recognize the authority of the persons who tell them. They do not look only for advice, they look for command and feel the more secure for being subject to it. Their situation is not as both the Utilitarians and the Contract theorists have sometimes described it; they do not learn to put up with authority because experience teaches them that in the long run they have more to gain than to lose by doing so. They are not by nature free and by convention subject to government. They come to aspire to freedom as they come to recognize authority, by learning to form purposes and to pursue them in an orderly world, a world which is both social and material. They recognize authority long before they are capable of appreciating its usefulness, and it is within a social order inconceivable without authority that they acquire the needs and the claims for whose sake they seek to limit authority.

To do what you are told by someone whose authority you recognize is neither to consent[1] to his authority nor to be coerced by him. No doubt, you may sometimes recognize his authority and yet be coerced by him; you may recognize that he is entitled to tell you what to do and yet obey him only because he threatens to punish you if you disobey. But quite often you do what you are told only because you recognize the authority of the person who tells

---

[1] That is to say, it is not consent in the sense of the word discussed in this book; it is not what we look for when we want to discover whether or not a government is representative.

you to do it; you would not have done it, had he not told you, and yet you are not coerced. You do it willingly enough, even though your doing it prevents your doing something else you wanted to do.

In any society, if men are friends or neighbours and none of them is recognized as having authority over the others, each is expected to consult the others before taking some action which is not admitted to be his private business and which deeply affects them. He acquires the right to act by getting their consent. He may even in this way acquire authority over them. In all societies there is a great deal of getting authority over equals with their consent, though this authority is usually very limited. Thus the idea that authority over equals derives from consent is familiar to men everywhere. They had no need of political theory to introduce it to them. The sophisticated idea, the invention of philosophers, is not that authority over equals derives from consent but that all human authority must do so because all men are equal until some of them have consented to the authority of others over them. But it makes no sense to say of men either that they are equal or that they are unequal unless they are in society together, unless there are social (and therefore also) moral relations between them. In all societies, there is both authority which derives from the consent of those subject to it and authority which does not. In many societies, the authority deriving from consent is ephemeral and limited, and its exercise is not elaborate. It is not enduring and is scarcely organized; it lasts for the duration of a hunt or an expedition, or for as long as it takes to carry out some project which involves both co-operation and subordination. It is not the organized and extensive authority which we call political, and it is not patriarchal.

Men who are equals are apt to resent fiercely the attempt of any one of their number to order them about unless they have given him authority to do so; that is to

say, unless they have consented to obey him and thereby
made him their superior. But from this we cannot conclude
that, where there is government by consent, obedience
is apt to be more willing and coercion less frequent than
where there is not. For what men resent is the attempt to
exercise an authority over them which they do not admit is
rightful. There is no evidence that they obey more willingly
where the authority whose rightfulness they admit derives
from their consent than where it does not. Let us agree
with the Utilitarians that coercion in itself is evil and ought
therefore to be avoided as far as it can be, but let us not go
on to say that, other things being equal, government by
consent is the best sort of government because it avoids
coercion more than the others do.

If to coerce a man is to make him do what he does not
want to do by threatening to hurt him unless he does it,
it is by no means obvious that the government of slaves
involves greater coercion than the government of the free.
It all depends on the attitude of the governed. If they
are respectful of authority and docile, there is little need
to coerce them. Bossuet thought the English of his day
almost ungovernable, so enamoured had they become of the
doctrine that all rightful authority derives from the consent
of the governed. This belief, which to him seemed absurd,
had made them suspicious of all government, and therefore peculiarly difficult to govern. It is unquestioned
authority, he thought, that weighs least heavily on those
subject to it. Bossuet's opinions about the English are
perhaps no more worthy of respect than the opinions of
de Gaulle, but it is worth noticing that even an absolute
government can be less coercive of its subjects than a
government by consent. Whether it is so or not must depend
greatly on the aspirations of the people and on what they
expect of their rulers.

There have been primitive peoples whose rulers have
had only a limited authority not derived from consent.

Such peoples have often been quick to resent any attempt of their rulers to extend their authority. They have been jealous of their freedom and yet have never thought of themselves as having the right to decide who shall rule them and what their rulers may justly require of them. When resisting their rulers, they have appealed to tradition without its ever occurring to them to argue that authority is legitimate only if it is exercised to protect the rights or to promote the interests of the people subject to it, who must be final judges as to whether or not it is so exercised. Among such peoples there is often very little governmental coercion, for the simple reason that there is very little organized government. Grown men are almost never coerced and are seldom commanded, though other kinds of pressure are put upon them to get them to carry out their obligations should they feel disinclined to do so. Authority weighs much more lightly on them than it does on the citizens of even the most democratic of modern states. If they were required to do what the Swiss or the English or the Americans today have to do at the bidding of government officials, they would think themselves terribly oppressed.

It is only among people who have come to believe that government ought to be by consent of the governed that its not being so makes it oppressive in their eyes. How then do they come to have this belief? Why do they not have it in so many primitive communities, though they bitterly resent what they consider to be abuses of authority? The wisdom of Bossuet notwithstanding, some of the peoples least easy to govern—simple mountain peoples—have never aspired to government by consent; they have merely cherished their freedom and have been quicker than others to disobey or to resist their rulers in its defence.

It is not until people require a great deal of their rulers that it comes to matter greatly to them that these rulers should govern with their consent. But the more they require of their rulers, the more their rulers require of them; the more extensive the machinery of government and the more numerous the laws and the orders that rain down upon them. The claim that government should be by consent of the governed usually arises as government grows more powerful, elaborate, extensive, and busy. This is by no means the only condition of its arising but it is one of the most important.

If we look at the countries where government by consent flourishes, we notice three things about them. They are countries where social and economic change is rapid, where government is growing more centralized and more busy, and where the individual thinks of himself as having the right to choose a career suited to his talents and his tastes.

No doubt, there is always in all countries some change, social and economic, but it may be so slow as to be almost imperceptible. Customs change, perhaps greatly over a long period of time, but little notice is taken of their doing so. And what change is noticed is mostly deplored as a falling off from the old established and only proper ways. The idea that the social order is something that men can change the better to suit their aspirations is altogether lacking. Men do not think of themselves as makers of law but as followers of it. The business of their rulers, as even their rulers see it, is not to decide what rules are to be enforced but to ensure that men do what has always been required of them, what justice and custom demand.

As men come gradually to think of the law as man-made and as alterable to suit changing circumstances, their attitude towards their rulers, towards the persons whose office it is to declare the law and apply it, slowly changes. They cease to look upon them as mere guardians of a law which no more expresses their will than it does the will of their subjects and they begin to see them as makers of the law who impose their will on others. When men keep the law, they no longer see themselves as doing what has always been done, what is proper and unquestionable, nor yet as simply obeying the commands of God. It seems to them that they are obeying not so much God as other men, and they begin to ask themselves why they should do so. They feel the need to ensure that the rules they are required to obey are to their advantage and not only to the advantage of their rulers. As it is brought home to them that to declare the law is virtually to make it, they come to think it important that the men who declare the law should be responsible to them for what they do. There thus arises the claim that those who declare (or make) the law derive their authority from the people required to obey them, from the community whose spokesmen or representatives they are. I speak here deliberately of what is in fact a complicated process, differing considerably from country to country, as if it were everywhere simple and steady. I speak not as an historian but as a political theorist trying to make use of some of the lessons of history.

The idea of law-making as the prime business of government is peculiar to societies which are changing fast and are aware that they are doing so. In Europe it became a commonplace among political theorists only in the seventeenth century. Hobbes defined law as command; it is 'to every subject, those rules which the commonwealth hath commanded him by word, writing, or other sufficient sign of the will, to make use of'. The legislator, be he one man or an assembly, is the sovereign, the possessor of supreme authority, because it is he 'that maketh the law'.[1] Locke also thought of the legislature as the supreme branch of government. Both Hobbes and Locke argued that the makers of law derive their authority to make it from their subjects; they thought of the people as conferring the right to make laws on whoever possessed that right. It is true that Hobbes was an apologist for absolute government

[1] Hobbes, *Leviathan*, Blackwell edition, p. 173.

and that even Locke sometimes spoke of consent in such a way as to suggest that every effective government has the consent of its subjects. Hobbes tried to use the idea of a social contract to reach conclusions distasteful to other users of the idea, and Locke resorted to strange arguments in the attempt to avoid extreme conclusions. They neither of them spoke of representative government as we do now. But they did assimilate the idea of consent to the idea of covenant or contract, and therefore gave to the doctrine that political authority derives from the consent of the governed implications that were more democratic and individualist than they were themselves aware of. I fasten upon their theories, not to subject them to criticism, but to illustrate my point, that two ideas emerged at about the same time in a society aware that it was changing fast: the idea that the prime business of government is to make law and the idea that political authority, to be legitimate, must somehow be conferred upon its possessors by the persons subject to it. Hobbes and Locke were easily the most influential political theorists of their century, and I take notice of what is common to their theories.

In some primitive societies, men are quick to resent any attempt of their rulers to require more of them than custom allows; they value their independence and hate to be ordered about. They are in one sense the freest of men, if we compare them, not just with slaves or serfs or with the subjects of an absolute ruler, but even with the citizens of a liberal democracy. They are much less under command than men can be in any highly civilized and economically developed country. They are proud and sensitive and careful of one another's feelings. But they do not make upon one another and upon their rulers the claims that are made by the citizens of a liberal democracy. Their conception of freedom is in important respects different. They are not critics of the social order; they do not want it changed to conform to their ideals more fully; they do not claim the right to live as seems good to them provided they respect the same right in others and are ready to do what society must require of them if it is to give them what they require of it. The idea of self-realization, of some personal ideal to be attained by their own efforts, means nothing to them. True, they assert themselves, they are concerned for reputation and have a lively sense of honour, but their aspirations are conventional. They are born to the roles they play in the world. They do not choose an occupation or a way of life to suit their peculiar talents and tastes, and make no claim upon society that it should provide them with the opportunity to make such a choice. They are not self-discoverers and self-improvers. They are neither adventurers nor self-made men, for all their pride and independence. They expect no more of their rulers than that they should do their part to maintain the social order in which everyone takes custom and tradition for unquestioned guides. Their rulers are close to them and yet have little power to make them do what they require of them unless what they require is endorsed by their neighbours. In one sense of the word *consent*, their power derives from the general consent of the community much more than does the power of most civilized rulers. Yet the people do not claim the right to confer authority on them.

Today all societies are quickly changing and much governed. Everyone is controlled and directed to an extent unimagined by his ancestors only a few generations ago, and this control and direction are exercised for purposes and in ways which do not long remain unaltered. Everywhere men are acquiring ambitions which they cannot satisfy without a multitude of services provided for them at public expense. They depend on government as never before, and yet the education they must have if they are to do the work now open to them inevitably makes them critical and demanding. They are taught to believe in *progress* which is represented to them as a liberating influence. They are told that they have opportunities their parents never had, and are urged to make the best of their talents. Their rulers, even when they subject them to the harshest discipline and impose heavy sacrifices on them, speak to them of their rights. They claim to be their agents, to be carrying out their will. They boast that their authority derives from the consent of the people.

We are amazed when we contemplate the world we now live in. Governments were never more often or more widely oppressive than they are today, and never more insistent that they were acting with the consent of the people subject to them. They could not demand of their subjects what they now demand, unless they claimed to be liberating them, and they could hardly claim to be doing that unless they claimed also to be acting with their consent. Rousseau, a recluse with a taste for paradox, might speak of citizens being forced to be free, but no government can afford to use such words today even though it drives its subjects as no government could do in Rousseau's time.

The claim made by these harsh governments that they are liberating their peoples is not altogether false. They are, in many ways, enlarging their opportunities. They are also changing their aspirations so that customs which used not to be restrictive have now come to be so and the attack upon them is felt to be a breaking of shackles. The young are taught science and are therefore made familiar with the scientific method, which tests hypotheses and rejects them when the facts are against them. No matter how severe the disciplines imposed from above, governments cannot achieve the aims they now set themselves except by developing capacities and encouraging hopes in their subjects which are incompatible with their being mere instruments. It may be nonsense to speak of forcing people to be free, but it is not nonsense to suggest that they can be so driven that the rights precious to the liberal and the democrat come at last to be precious to them. They may learn slowly in a hard school to value certain kinds of freedom and a certain kind of government.

I do not say that material progress is impossible without awakening in men aspirations which are best satisfied in a society where there is government by consent together with the liberties which that type of government entails. I suggest only that in our world, as it happens to be, material progress has brought and still brings such aspirations with it. The historian alone can explain why this is so, if indeed it is so. It is not to be explained by reflecting in the abstract on human needs and capacities and the necessary conditions of material progress. It is conceivable that in some other world, knowing nothing of such related and yet rival creeds as liberalism, Marxism, and nationalism, there could be powerful governments skilfully promoting the rapid growth of material wealth without encouraging any such aspirations.

I dare not predict that these aspirations will be satisfied. I am not a Marxist; I do not think it inevitable, nor even highly probable, that what I think desirable will come to pass. It may be that the material progress which in our world happens to bring these aspirations with it also puts obstacles, social and cultural, in their way. But, even if we allow that it is so, we can still say: Given these aspirations, there is a powerful case to be made for government by consent.

Unfortunately, it is not the case made in this old-fashioned book. Nor have I attempted to make it in this new postscript. I have only given reasons why, in my opinion, it could be made in a world in which all the social and political creeds competing with the liberal creed are ideologically closely related with it. The West gave birth to them all, almost in the same litter.

J. P. P.

Oxford 1967